The FRANKLIN DELANO ROOSEVELT Memorial

CHRONICLE BOOKS

SAN FRANCISCO

The FRANKLIN
DELANO
ROOSEVELT Memorial

MEMORIAL DESIGNER
LAWRENCE HALPRIN

SPECIAL FDR MEMORIAL EDITION

Produced for Parks & History Association

Partners in Education with the National Park Service

For more information: www.parksandhistory.org

(202) 472 3083

Grateful acknowledgment is made for the following:

"Ode to Walt Whitman" from *Burning City* by Stephen Vincent Benet. Copyright © 1935 by Stephen Vincent Benet. Copyright renewed 1963 by Thomas C. Benet, Rachel Benet Lewis, and Stephanie Benet Mahin. Reprinted with permission of Brandt & Brandt Literary Agency, Inc.

Photo Credits:

All illustrations are from the archives of the Office of Lawrence Halprin, Inc., except the following: *Franklin D. Roosevelt Library:* pages 5, 32, 33, 41, 51 bottom, 55, 56, 60/61, 90, 96, 97, 104, 108, 115, 119, 122. *Library of Congress, Prints and Photographs Division,* pages and reproduction numbers: 40/41, LC-USF33-2407-M-2; 47, USA7-18242; 65, USF34-16907-E; 71, USF34-18667-L; 82, US262-69171. *Keystone Press Agency:* 50. *National Archives:* 51 top, 54, 63, 64 bottom, 68, 93, 106/107, 130, 131. *Robert Graham* (FDR First Inaugural, 1997): 52/53. *Brown Brothers:* 64 top. *Courtesy of* Sydney Janis Gallery, N.Y.: 70,72. *Archive/Popperfoto:* 73. *Archive Photos:* 86, 88. *General Services Administration, Public Buildings Service, Fine Arts Collection:* 84. *The New York Times,* copyright © 1939 by The New York Times Co., reprinted by permission: 87. *The Boeing Historical Archives:* 90/91. *Diane Smook,* copyright © 1996: 105. *AP/World Wide Photos:* 111.

Library of Congress Cataloging-in-Publication Data available.
ISBN 0-8118-2935-9.

Book Design by Tenazas Design *San Francisco*

Printed in Hong Kong.

Distributed in Canada by Raincoast Books
8680 Cambie Street
Vancouver, B.C. V6P 6M9

10 9 8 7 6 5 4 3 2 1

Chronicle Books
85 Second Street
San Francisco, CA 94105

www.chroniclebooks.com

Table of Contents

My early life was intertwined with the influences of Franklin Delano Roosevelt as far back as I can remember.

I was born and raised in New York City, and I experienced the years of the Great Depression with my family first-hand. When I graduated high school at age sixteen, FDR was running for his first term as president. It was 1932 and the Depression was getting worse throughout the country. I spent some vacations working with coal miners in Pennsylvania, and others working for the Civilian Conservation Corps, a New Deal program which was created by FDR in 1933. I remember the issues and innovations of FDR's presidency.

When the United States entered World War II, my graduate schooling at Harvard School of Design accelerated and I volunteered for the navy. I had absolutely no question about our need to fight the war, and I was anxious to join. I spent several years thereafter on a destroyer in the Pacific. Toward the end of the war, my destroyer, the USS *Morris* DD 417 was cut in half by a kamikaze plane while we were covering the landings at Okinawa.

I will never forget the moment our radio announced that President Roosevelt was dead. Although we were a fighting ship with years under combat, there wasn't a dry eye among the crew. We felt we had lost not only our commander in chief, but also a man who had become a warm, beloved presence in our lives.

Ten years after the end of World War II, in August 1955, a joint resolution of Congress established the Franklin Delano Roosevelt Memorial Commission to build a memorial to this great president. In September 1959 a site was reserved in West Potomac Park by Public Law 86-214.

The commission could not have known that finding an approvable design would take almost twenty years. The first design competition was held in 1960, and 547 submissions were received. The chosen design was abandoned in 1965 in the face of public controversy, and a subsequent design was also rejected by the Commission of Fine Arts in 1967. The selection process languished until the spring of 1974, when the FDR Commission decided to hold another competition by invitation. My proposal was selected.

THE DESIGN PROCESS that started in 1974 and ended with the opening of the Memorial in 1997 was long and intense and was influenced by many commissions, many groups, and many people both in and out of government. Early on, I grasped the importance of this intricate and interactive process. The path has taken many twists and turns. We have had many major presentations, we have acquired numerous approvals, we have suffered through numerous shifts in personnel. It has been a long and fascinating journey.

The FDR Memorial Commission and particularly its chairmen—Senator Mark O. Hatfield, Senator Daniel K. Inouye, Representative Eugene Keogh, and Senator Claude Pepper—have been an inspiration for me to work with over the years. Eugene Keogh was chairman when I first entered the picture in 1974. He was instrumental in beginning and guiding the design competition and design process through its early approvals. Senator Claude Pepper, who had been an early New Dealer and a protégé of FDR, accepted the chairman's duties at a particularly slow point in the commission's history. Despite his advanced years and declining health, Senator Pepper succeeded in activating the appropriations process so that construction could get under way. Leaving his hospital bed to make his last official trip to the Capitol, he appeared before the House Appropriations Committee. He further advanced the project by presenting his plea for support to President George Bush, who visited the hospital during the senator's final days.

After Senator Pepper's death, the chairmanship was shared by Senators Mark O. Hatfield and Daniel K. Inouye with tremendous dedication. Both of these men have devoted enormous time and commitment to this effort to honor Franklin Delano Roosevelt. Senator Inouye, a Democrat, fought in Italy and France during World War II, earning a multitude of medals and citations. Senator Hatfield, a Republican, served as a lieutenant j.g. in the U.S. Navy during the war. He witnessed battles at Iwo Jima and Okinawa and was among the first U.S. servicemen to enter Hiroshima following the atomic bombing. These men have been incredibly strong allies of the Memorial, sometimes under very difficult conditions. The Memorial owes them its very existence.

In the beginning, any design project of this complexity is an exercise in three-dimensional imagination. The designer, starting with the basic idea and the building site, must imagine what it will eventually look like in each and every one of its parts. That, however, is only one piece of the process. Beyond that, and perhaps most importantly, it is necessary to think deeply about what you, as a designer, would like people to feel as they experience the space. To do that, a designer must in some way preview the project, sensing the shapes and forms of spaces, the pacing and rhythm of movement. He must be able to hear, smell, and touch the intended place. In this way the designer can expand his intentions and refine the choreography and kinesthetic of the place that is to be.

The writing of this book has given me an opportunity to engage in a new aspect of the design process. With the construction of the Memorial completed, I can review and explain why and how I have designed the Memorial. I can take this opportunity to show how the history of the Roosevelt era is expressed in the stone, water, and bronze of the Memorial.

During the writing of this book, I visited the Memorial site to monitor construction. As I watched the vision for the Memorial become a reality, I was reminded of all I wanted to express. Reading the inscriptions, I remembered why they were chosen. Visiting the bronze foundries, I was reminded of the workshop sessions with the sculptors. Watching the giant cranes install the monolithic stones, I recalled my many visits to the quarry to select each block.

It is my hope that with this book I can transmit the reasons behind the design and that, as a result, the Memorial will become more alive for all who visit.

As I finalize the creative process of writing this book, I am also reminded of those who helped make it possible. I want to thank Jay Schaefer, at Chronicle Books, for his encouragement, his subtle insights, and his professional evaluations as I progressed. I would like to note my appreciation of Lynne Creighton, who toiled endlessly and with great patience selecting and tracking historical photographs. I need to express my gratitude to Don Noll of Cold Springs Granite for his dialogues with me throughout the process of developing both the Memorial and the book. He has helped me throughout the years of this project to understand the nature and quarrying of granite. Lucille Tenazas deserves great thanks for her elegant book design. She has transmuted conceptual ideas, words, and images into a beautiful and understandable graphic form. And in particular, I want to thank Dee Mullen of my office, who has stood by my side on this project for the twenty-two years it has taken to evolve. I want to acknowledge her help in articulating the process and editing the words and graphics that have captured the essence of my meanings.

Lawrence Halprin

In this view of the FDR
Memorial site across the
Tidal Basin, the Washington
Monument rises in the
foreground and the Jefferson
Memorial lies off to the left.
The Potomac flows in the
background.

Introduction

THE FRANKLIN DELANO ROOSEVELT MEMORIAL celebrates one of the four great presidents of our 220-year history as a country. The first was George Washington, who led our struggle for independence. Next came Thomas Jefferson, who was a primary author of the Declaration of Independence and who, perhaps more importantly, unified the country from coast to coast. President Abraham Lincoln, who sought to give liberty to all of our citizens while keeping us united, was our third great president.

Now, as the twentieth century draws to a close, it is time to celebrate President Franklin Delano Roosevelt.

Franklin Roosevelt guided the country through a series of terrible crises on both the national and international level. He led the United States to a new level of preeminence in the world. He was also our first modern president, and the only one to win four terms of office. FDR served as president from 1933 to 1945, a twelve-year period which proved to be a turning point for the twentieth century. It was a time that changed the world.

Each one of these four presidents was destined to be honored by a unique memorial in our nation's capital. I was honored to accept the challenge of designing the fourth memorial, and I have endeavored, over a period of more than twenty years, to evolve an appropriate way, in a modern form, to celebrate this remarkable man.

Earlier presidential memorials had taken their inspiration from forms of the past. They harkened back to classical Greek, Roman, and even Egyptian imagery. The Lincoln and Jefferson Memorials are symbolic objects in the landscape, beautifully hollowed out tombs surrounded by marble columns. Both contain a classically serene image of their president as an icon. I wanted to find a new approach which could express the unique characteristics of FDR's presidency. And it seemed to me that the most remarkable characteristic was the multitude of crises he encountered and overcame.

This image of FDR was used as his campaign poster during the 1936 presidential election. The photo was taken in Charlotte, North Carolina, on September 10, 1936.

I felt that the repetition of this classical motif, the creation of another architectural object, would be inappropriate, no matter how beautifully designed. It would not represent the challenge of a new world in the making. I therefore began to look for a form that was more emotional and more expressive; a form that would express universally shared human experiences with the informality and complexity of modern life.

The design concept I was searching for would need to provide a venue to highlight both the experience of living through the FDR presidency and also the profound influence he had on our nation and on the world. FDR rallied the country and enlisted the aid of myriad forces to overcome the poverty, the economic failures, and the natural disasters he encountered upon taking office. He provided the impetus to develop a public support network for millions of Americans caught in the depths of unemployment. He foresaw international crisis and provided leadership to a country threatened by the numbing shock waves of war in Europe and the Pacific. And, through it all, FDR always kept his sights on the search for a lasting peace throughout the world.

These unprecedented historical challenges, following on the heels of one another, presented me with an enormous problem. How was I to portray this multitude of historically important events? How was I to explain the intensity of resolve necessary to overcome them? This was at the center of the design dilemma I faced when I was chosen to design the Franklin Delano Roosevelt Memorial in 1974.

Before the design process actually began, I thought a great deal about the reasons for having memorials and about what lies at the core of our emotional need for such monuments. All cultures from primitive times to the present have celebrated their gods, their heroes, and their major events through memorials. Some religions have created monuments in the form of profound writings such as the Bible or the Koran. Some cultures have cast their monuments in the physical form of megaliths such as Stonehenge in England or of classical temples such as at the Acropolis and Delphi in Greece. Each civilization has expressed much of its own character through the forms in which it cast its great monuments.

MEMORIALS ARE ARCHETYPAL. They speak of life's meanings, of value systems held in common, of significant challenges and events in the history of a tribe or a nation. Memorials speak to us over the ages. They transmit universal truths and experience; they pass the torch of meaning from one generation to the next.

When I started the design process for the FDR Memorial, I thought of the feelings I hoped people would have as they walked through it. I thought of the ambiance of the country during those years, and I wanted the Memorial experience to capture the character and quality of that era for visitors. Finally, I thought of how President Roosevelt defined and directed this country at that pivotal time in our development.

In the FDR Memorial I hoped to evoke as many emotions and approaches as I could. I wanted the experience of this Memorial to reveal the dramatic story that unfolded during President Roosevelt's four terms, the twelve years when he was president of the United States. His was a hero's journey—from the urgency of his first term of office and the New Deal, through his struggles to overcome the Great Depression, through the trauma of World War II, and finally to his search for an honorable and everlasting peace.

As I thought about our hopes for the Memorial and how I might achieve them through design, I realized that no one object, building, or statue could express the broad scope of those years. No single image could capture the multiplicity of events, challenges, difficulties, and successes. No simple statement could adequately express the achievements. Somehow I needed to evoke in each visitor, through his or her own experience of the Memorial, a deep and emotional understanding of how these years changed the lives of the people who lived through them.

I decided that only a slow-paced, personal experience, which would take place over sufficient time, could transmit the importance of this era to future generations.

I wanted this Memorial to be an EXPERIENTIAL HISTORY LESSON that people could grasp on their own as they walked through it.

In my own experience, I have been emotionally affected by a number of monuments—at the Acropolis in Athens, Ise Shrine in Japan, Delphi in Greece, and the Western Wall in Jerusalem. I noted that these all had a number of elements in common. They unfolded like voyages, based on movement along prescribed routes; their entrances were welcoming and signified importance; and pathways led onward from the special gateways in linear progressions. At each site, there were also stopping places along the way, which allowed for time to contemplate or meditate on experiences felt along the route.

The stops on my favorite memorial pathways always came naturally. They were associated with views, events, sculptural objects, places to sit, and magnificent landforms. There was always something with which to interact physically, emotionally, intellectually, or spiritually. These processional paths always offered variations in pace through their design, yet there was always a consistent sense of physical and emotional choreography. Visitors were drawn on through a sequence of experiences—some calm, some intense—and there was a pervasive sense of drama. At the end of such experiences, I felt that in a profound way I emerged deeply changed. I felt that I had come through a focused slice of life that affected me intensely and emotionally.

I wanted the FDR Memorial to capture this narrative quality, and the idea of a processional passage through a series of historically charged events began to dominate my early thoughts regarding the design. My earliest sketches in 1974 express this idea.

THE FRANKLIN DELANO ROOSEVELT MEMORIAL COMMISSION,
which had been established by Congress to act as client for the Memorial, had developed a set of criteria that guided my design process. The guidelines were:

1   That the landscape solution harmonize with the beauty of the existing parklike setting.
2   That waterplay be a significant element of the memorial environment.
3   That no major structure dominate the site.
4   That an image or images of Roosevelt were appropriate.
5   That the existing recreational areas be retained.

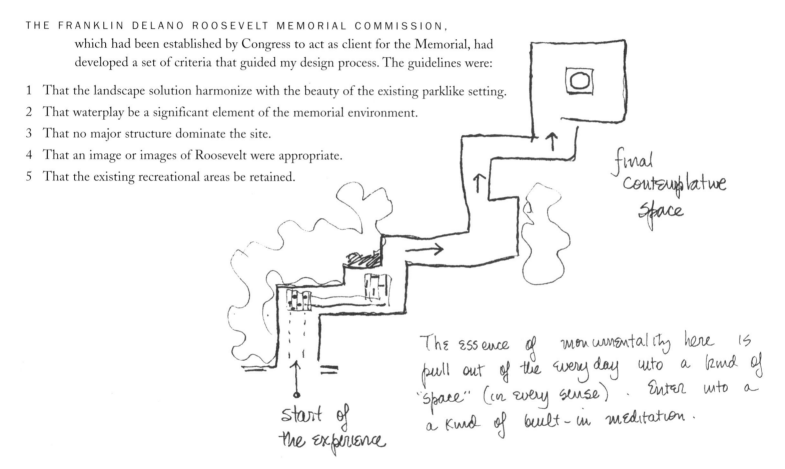

final
contemplative
space

The essence of monumentality here is pull out of the every day into a kind of "space" (in every sense). Enter into a a kind of built-in meditation.

start of
the experience

It was clear from this mandate that both the Cherry Walk, which had become a major visual symbol of spring in Washington, and the athletic fields to the west of the Tidal Basin had to be retained. This seemed most appropriate. Franklin Roosevelt had been vitally involved in athletics as a young man, and multitudes of young government aides are drawn to this recreational area so close to their workplaces. Coupled with the need to retain these amenities was a need to separate daily recreational routines from the contemplative, spiritual space of the Memorial. I began to think of these distinct areas as the secular everyday spaces and the sacred memorial space.

The Memorial site lies beyond the athletic fields, in the distance under the elm trees.

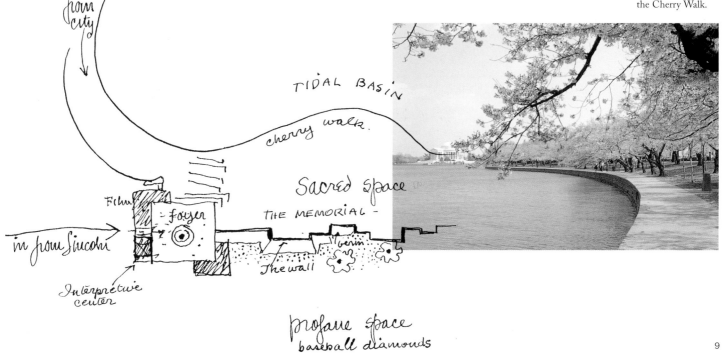

athletic fields

↓ The wall

berm   memorial

In order to make my early processional concept work, I had to first decide how to differentiate between the sacred and secular uses on the peninsula. I accomplished this by evolving the idea of a wall that would separate the two functions and allow them to proceed simultaneously. The athletic fields could have their own sound and activity and not interrupt the special sense of place and the spiritual, contemplative character that I wanted the Memorial to inspire.

Once the idea of the wall as a linear divider emerged, many other concepts fell into place. The walls of the Memorial allowed me the opportunity to develop an appropriately formal entrance or gateway that would signal a visitor's arrival at an important, monumental place. This gateway marks the beginning of the FDR Memorial experience.

The long, linear character of the wall also paralleled the Tidal Basin and the Cherry Walk. It allowed the Memorial to focus eastward toward monumental Washington and the great significant views across the inlet—of the Washington Monument and the Jefferson and Lincoln Memorials. These views and the way they orient the Memorial into historic Washington are an important element in the overall design. They underscore the greatness of all four presidents.

This view of the Jefferson Memorial may be seen from the Cherry Walk.

from city

TIDAL BASIN

cherry walk.

Sacred space

THE MEMORIAL -

Fchu

foyer

in from Lincoln

Interpretive center

berm

The wall

profane space
baseball diamonds

I also recognized that the wall would become the spine of the Memorial.

And like a spine, it would not only establish physical shape, but could also support and carry the other major elements which would give content to the Memorial—sculpture, quotations, fountains, and plantings.

During this same time period, I realized that the complexity of this historic Memorial would need a strong sense of order. FDR's presidency was not smooth and flowing. It was punctuated by a tumultuous series of events. It needed chapters, like a novel, and FDR's presidency divided naturally into four chapters, his four terms of office.

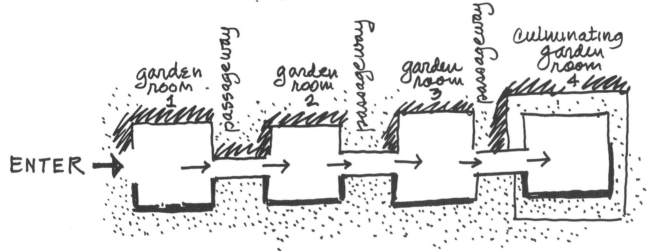

The long processional and its defining wall was therefore segmented into four outdoor rooms. Each room would be devoted to one of FDR's terms in office and would tell the story of what happened to the country and the world during that period. The number *four* began to set a basic rhythm in and around the Memorial—four presidential memorials, four terms in office, four outdoor rooms.

Washington, D.C.

The focus of the design process had to expand at this point and take into account the larger physical context for the Memorial. The original plan for the federal city was initiated by President Washington in 1791. When the First Constitutional Congress met in 1789, northern delegates favored Wrights Ferry, Pennsylvania, as the location for the federal city, and southern delegates suggested Georgetown on the Potomac River. The compromise site on the Potomac, south of Georgetown, was selected in 1790.

Thomas Jefferson, who was a distinguished amateur architect, was asked by George Washington to advise him on the layout of a plan for the site. They both wanted a plan whose basic strength and sense of monumental place would withstand the unpredictable changes of succeeding years. Jefferson, joined by the French-born artist and engineer Pierre Charles L'Enfant and the surveyor Andrew Ellicott, developed a carefully gridded matrix for the city with an overlay of diagonal avenues and points of importance. The main features of the plan were a central pedestrian mall, a special location for the capitol on Jenkins Hill, and a special place for the president's house with a view south to the river. This magnificent plan owes much of its monumentality to the influences of European precedents at Versailles, Paris, and the Tuileries Gardens as well as the masterworks of André Le Nôtre.

This layout still serves as the basic skeleton of the capital city. But for a hundred years or so after its inception, a confusion of additional plans, modifications, and inconsistencies plagued the development of the city, until, in the early 1900s, a Senate group headed by Senator James McMillan set out to reclaim the strength of the plan under the aegis of President Theodore Roosevelt. The result of the work, a brilliant plan which extended the vision of Pierre L'Enfant, was achieved by designers Daniel Burnham, Frederick Law Olmsted Jr., and Charles F. McKim. This plan, the McMillan Plan, was presented and approved in 1901. It established the location of three new memorials to join the existing Washington Monument. They would eventually be dedicated to Abraham Lincoln, Thomas Jefferson, and, finally, Franklin Delano Roosevelt.

With the concept and thematic approach established, I had to form the shape of the Memorial in such a way as to conform exactly to the existing site and this Memorial's relationship to the McMillan Plan (nicknamed the KITE PLAN), whose geometry dominates monumental Washington. In some ways, the two were incompatible. The Kite Plan identifies a point halfway between the Lincoln and Jefferson Memorials, with axial sightlines radiating to them as well as to the Washington Monument. The identifying point implied that the FDR Memorial would be a simple, structural, geometric form—either a circle or square. Many assumed that it would be an object like the other three presidential memorials, probably cast in a classic mold.

The idea of a processional design reaching outward in the landscape was a surprising innovation and one which had not yet been attempted.

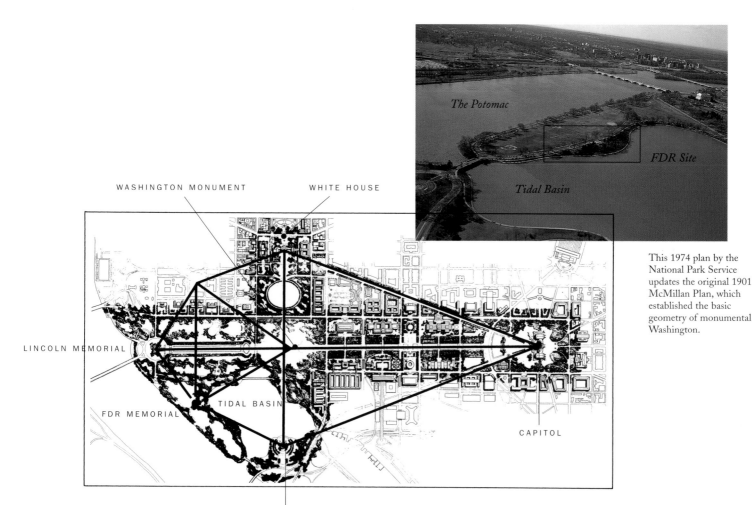

WASHINGTON MONUMENT   WHITE HOUSE

The Potomac

FDR Site

Tidal Basin

LINCOLN MEMORIAL

FDR MEMORIAL

TIDAL BASIN

CAPITOL

JEFFERSON MEMORIAL

This 1974 plan by the
National Park Service
updates the original 1901
McMillan Plan, which
established the basic
geometry of monumental
Washington.

I devoted much thought to integrating the idea of a formal, contained point on the McMillan Plan
with the shape of a processional. After considerable study, I proposed placing the entrance to the
Memorial on the exact point that had been designated by the McMillan Plan. The Memorial would
then extend visually toward the Jefferson Memorial, linking the two and strengthening the
geometry of the overall plan.

As a landform, the site itself (the peninsula) possessed a very dominant geometry, established by the
curvilinear form of the Tidal Basin to the east and the straight edge of the Potomac River and Ohio
Drive to the west. In addition, a linear planting of vaselike American elms bordered the eastern
road, and myriad Japanese cherry trees sloped down to the edge of the Tidal Basin.

The cherry trees with their magnificent blossoms had become a beautiful destination for many thousands of spring visitors to Washington, D.C. Now they would add their beauty to the Memorial and become a major feature for its parklike setting. It seemed mandatory to preserve as many of the existing plantings as possible. Yet no direct straight line for the processional (and its granite spine) could weave through the loose location of the existing trees, which had been planted in an informal pattern in the early part of the century.

After studying this problem, I decided upon a design which stepped forward deliberately from the Memorial's entrance on a diagonal toward the Jefferson Memorial. This framework allowed the Memorial to conform to the site *and* fit into the McMillan Plan. It also provided the opportunity to form four outdoor rooms, like knots on a rope, and link them with narrower garden passageways.

Following the edge of the Tidal Basin gave a rhythmic line to the wall, which started in the cup of the basin and stretched outward, like a belvedere, to the rounded end of the peninsula.

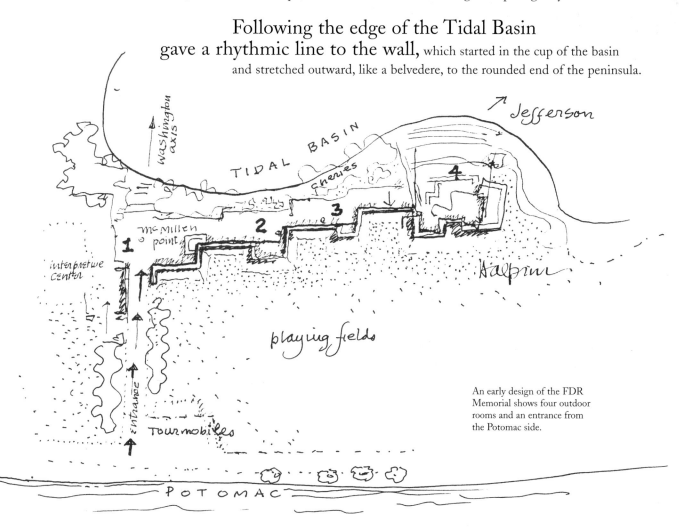

An early design of the FDR Memorial shows four outdoor rooms and an entrance from the Potomac side.

At the Cold Spring Granite quarry, cranes and cable saws are used for removing the massive pieces of granite.

Stone

The choice of the stone for the Memorial wall was the next issue at hand. Franklin Delano Roosevelt had an intense interest in building. As a farmer and good husbandman, he had continually sought to improve the Roosevelt estate at Hyde Park, New York; he was an aficionado of architecture and personally oversaw the building of a stone-walled library at the estate and the development of Val-Kill, a retreat for Eleanor. In all of these endeavors he was particularly fascinated by stone. He preferred the reddish gray fieldstones typically found in New England. It was similar to the stone that had been used by Frederick Law Olmsted in his designs for Central Park, and it can still be seen in many of the townhouses in Manhattan as well.

The wall was to be a very dominant element in the Memorial, and as we began to search for the appropriate stone, I hoped to find a New England quarry that would be able to provide a similarly colored stone in large sizes and large quantities. We found we had to look farther, however, because the original quarries had been shut down and the color and texture of the stone that we wanted was not available. So we enlarged our search and finally found a granite that we admired at the Cold Spring quarries on the border between South Dakota and Minnesota. The granite is called *Carnelian*.

This Carnelian granite sets the tone of the Memorial.

It has a presence that carries an enormous feeling of deep-rooted security. When quarried from the mother rock, it splits off with a rough but uniform face which does not feel formal when set up as a wall; it feels as if it's part of the earth.

Its character and color are distinctly different from the white marble of the other memorials and buildings in Washington. It projects an earthy, land-oriented quality that is more of our time, and it articulates more of Roosevelt's personality as well as that of his home. The stone is hard and durable, uniform in its grain and, like all granite, diverse in its makeup of igneous feldspar, quartz, and mica. It will last for centuries.

The dominant color of this stone is a deep, earthy, reddish gray with some variations, and it changes in the light because of the flecks of mica. When the granite face is split, the reddish color, with its darker dapples and sparkling chips of mica, are striking yet subdued, and the overall impression is of quiet power and dignity.

The method of taking cut stone out of the quarry is remarkable, and my growing understanding of the process profoundly influenced the final shaping and finishes of the granite in the Memorial.

In many ways, this stone quarrying process is primitive, as people have been making building blocks from quarried stone for their places of remembrance and worship for ages.

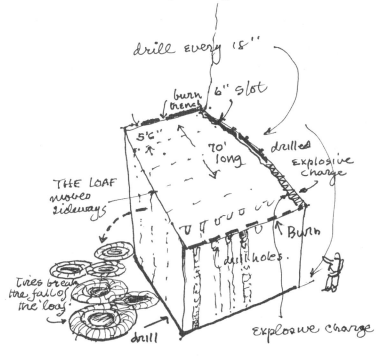

A view into the quarry, as the granite loafs are removed from the base rock.

The first step is to remove what is called a *loaf* from the base rock. A loaf is usually ten to twenty feet deep and can be as long as seventy feet. It is released from the bedrock by drilling holes for explosive charges in the rock and exploding it from the matrix. As the loaf separates, its fall is softened by great rubber tires—in older times the fall was softened by tree boughs or sand.

hook
pull

blow whistle 3x - change
moves slab out 6" to 1'6"

GRANITE SLICE.
Typical size
5'6 × 5'6 × 8'6"
in the quarry

17
3'0"
5'6"

17'6"

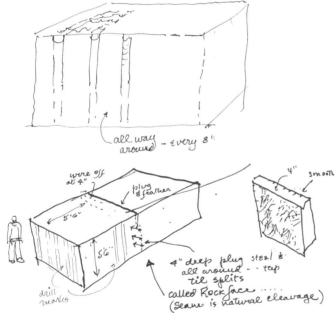

all way
around - every 8"

were off
at 4"

plug
& feather

4" smooth

5'6"

5'6"

drill
marks

4" deep plug steel &
all around - - tap
til splits
called Rock face
(seam is natural cleavage)

Measuring thirty feet long
and 6 feet high before it is
shaped, this stone is nicknamed
"the mother stone."

Once the loaf is free, it is gradually sliced
and/or split, either by cutting or by having
steel plugs tapped and hammered around its
girth, depending on the desired finish. In most
architectural uses, granite and other stone
facing is cut into smooth pieces by rotating
great diamond-blade saws through thick
blocks. These pieces are then hung, from the
substructure of the building.

Vern Maile and Wally
Leither shape a wall stone
at the Cold Spring factory.

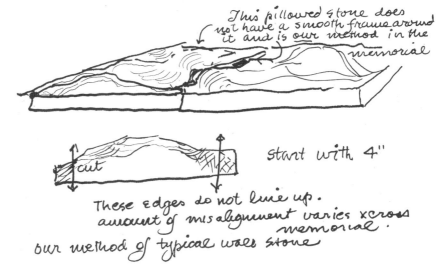

pitch off 4" drill marks from feather uniform perimeter

pillow

smooth frame around stone

uniform pillowing.

pillowed stone with frame around

In more complex building uses, particularly in lower, pedestrian-level facades, granite is often pillowed or split into a rougher surface. This pillowed effect is achieved by manufacturing a smooth frame around each piece, which allows the stones to fit together with their neighbors.

In the Memorial design, I chose a split-finish surface manufactured without a smooth frame. Because the roughness of the surface varies with the size of the stones, the FDR Memorial wall achieves the primitive feeling of stone emerging from the quarry. It is rough, ancient, and monumental in character.

This pillowed stone does not have a smooth frame around it and is our method in the memorial

cut

start with 4"

These edges do not line up. amount of misalignment varies across memorial.

our method of typical wall stone

I knew that throughout the Memorial the granite would have to perform a variety of tasks, and I was confident that the Carnelian finishes offered me this range. The basic stone on the wall would be split-finish. Most of the quotations would occur on a thermal finish, a surface which has been burned with torches at about 1,800 degrees Fahrenheit, to better accept sand-blasted letters. At certain locations, however, the finish would be rough and mountainous, and the letters would need to be carved by hand to give emphasis to FDR's most powerful statements. And the rugged, mountainous feeling would be carried even further in certain locations by the presence of great granite boulders. This potential variety was an aspect of the stone that gave me a multitude of design options. I knew that I could set the stones in the walls in a way that would produce an enormous range in emotional quality as people walked through the Memorial.

The scale and proportions of the wall, its height and overall length, were then studied exhaustively. I had many clay study models handcrafted at my studio in San Francisco. My primary intention was that the height of the wall should have a monumental quality. At the same time, however, it needed to be human in scale and not overwhelm the visitors who would interact with it. My design team and I vacillated between twelve and fourteen feet, finally settling on twelve. The twelve-foot height enabled us to set the stones in three-foot-high courses and stack them four courses high. Once again, the number four was prominent in the Memorial.

A faux Styrofoam granite wall section is constructed as a working model in Halprin's design office.

The three-foot-high coursing also reinforced the human scale since two courses, at six feet or midwall, was within the height range of an average person. That midwall range would carry much of the message of the Memorial in the form of quotations and sculptures, and the wall height therefore established a human baseline throughout the Memorial. At that point, our office became home to a twelve-foot-high Styrofoam wall which was painted to match the Carnelian granite. This faux wall was a constant companion, always available to keep us constantly aware of its proportions.

Halprin and John Benson
review a granite mock-up.
Carnelian granite is used
here with various examples
of carved inscriptions.

This wall in the third-term
room is a fine example of
the various stone sizes and
textures. It also includes a
quotation inscribed on
a thermal finished panel.

Meanwhile, at the Cold Spring quarry, they built a number of full-scale sections for us to study a variety of situations and techniques. Stone shapes, corners, buttresses, surface textures, carving requirements, ground connections, and many other issues were mocked-up and tested at the quarry. During frequent visits there, I decided that although the three-foot coursing should remain a consistent horizontal pattern, there would be times when stones should extend up to two courses in height. Those immense stones would break the normal patterning and emphasize the feeling of weight and strength. The horizontal scale of stones would also vary in a random pattern from two feet to ten or twelve feet. One stone we found at the quarry was approximately thirty feet long and six feet high. I noted that particular stone and decided that I would find a special place for it in the Memorial.

Eventually, 31,239 STONES, including pavers, were used in the Memorial. The pavers were designed in a repetitive random pattern that was easy to fabricate. But the layout of the 4,000 wall stones, which extend for 800 feet along the edge of the Memorial, required a unique design effort.

The wall could not be repetitive.

In order to reflect the emotional message we wanted to express, each of those stones had to be individually designed and fabricated by hand at the quarry!

Sculptors

By March 1976, the basic architectural scheme for the Memorial had been established, but the narrative content—the poetry, the imagery, the verbal messages—still needed to be integrated into what was so far only a spatial experience.

I knew that I could not take the physical plan of the Memorial any further without bringing decisions on the artwork into the picture. The art was a major element which could provide a number of new levels of enrichment to the Memorial.

I needed to begin working with the artists.

It had been clear to me from the beginning that any sculpture should be figurative. I knew that the architectural aspects of the Memorial would evoke feelings based on the overall environment, the vistas, and the relationship of spaces and materials. These elements evoked reactions much like those elicited by abstract sculptures. On the other hand, figurative sculpture of a high order can particularize and humanize a vision. It speaks not in a language of generalized gestures but of life's realities.

I had always assumed that the Memorial would include a likeness of Franklin Delano Roosevelt—probably as a focal point toward the end of the Memorial. The evolution of the procession idea, however, led naturally to the need for a progression of images, and the feeling that each of the outdoor rooms would probably contain several sculptures. Here was an opportunity to humanize the experience, give historical content to the Memorial, evoke some real appreciation in visitors of the tremendous impact these events had on the people who lived through them.

I had also come to the conclusion that all sculpture was to be in bronze. The Carnelian granite would not respond well to carved images, but I felt it would interact well with the color of the bronze. Compatibility was important, because I felt that the processional quality of the Memorial required that all sculpture be on or adjacent to the walls. The Memorial was to be a walking experience guided by a twelve-foot-high granite wall. The wall would define the Memorial's four outdoor rooms as well as the three passageways which linked them together.

As a result, the selection process for the sculptors was important. I had a number of artists in mind whose work was of the highest order and who seemed appropriate for the task, but in order to universalize and objectify that selection, I discussed my preferences with twelve experts in the field. I consulted with museum directors, gallery directors, critics, and members of the National Council of the Arts. This process expanded my original group of selectees, and I found myself with a list of recommendations that included twenty-seven prominent sculptors, several from abroad. The FDR Memorial Commission felt that it was desirable for all the artists to be from the United States, which eliminated the foreign artists; the list was further reduced when I added the requirement that, to be eligible, all artists must have considerable experience working on large-scale bronzes.

In July 1977, I took a trip to visit with the various artists left on the list. I wanted to see their studios, examine their working conditions, and interview them regarding their attitudes and their ability to take on a commission of this scale. I also needed to clarify for each of them the requirements for working on such a high-profile project, as well as the possible limitations and difficulties of working on an artistic commission that had multiple clients.

Halprin visits Leonard Baskin in his art studio in Leeds, Massachusetts.

I must say that the interviews and interactions with the sculptors during the creative selection process were among the most interesting and provocative of my life. It was exciting to explore the possibility for this Memorial with great artists. There were many concerns and many opinions regarding how symbolic art could best express to future generations these major historical events of the twentieth century and much discussion of how the artists would have to deal not only with me, but also with the clients and client representatives who reviewed these aesthetic areas.

Many of the artists I interviewed had never worked on commission. George Segal commented that he was used to working on "self-directed art," not "directed art." He wasn't sure if he would like this new way of working—of being given a subject for his art. A recurrent question from my notes of those visits dealt with the issue of artistic freedom. The question was posed in various ways, but it always came down to the issue of how much influence the multiplicity of individuals and commissions overseeing the project would have on decisions regarding the form and content of the artwork. This was a valid concern.

I had already encountered many commissions and governmental oversight agencies in my work on the project. I considered my primary client to be the Congress of the United States as represented by the Franklin Delano Roosevelt Memorial Commission. I was also, however, working with the National Park Service, which administers, manages, and maintains the monuments and memorials in the nation's capital, and with other agencies which had specific interests in water, power, traffic, fire issues, and so on. In addition to the usual give and take necessary for normal construction in this area, our project had the added complexity of art, quotations, and carvings. So we were also subject to the oversight groups which review all plans and artworks for Washington, D.C. The most demanding and important of them all is probably the Commission of Fine Arts.

As an architectural designer, I have developed an interactive method of working on public projects, and I have learned to expect such a process.

I have grown accustomed to it and I know that at times it can be incredibly creative and exhilarating.

Inevitably, however, it can also become difficult and demanding.

For the sculptors, this process was unusual, and it made frustrating demands upon them.

After twenty years, the basic concept and design has persevered, and it has benefited from the years of interaction. Carter Brown, chairman of the Fine Arts Commission, captured the outcome of the process best in the following statement, made at the end of a commission meeting on the final design: "I think this is one of the finest days in the history of the commission, to see how a kind of dialogue with a designer can take something which I thought was pretty darn good to begin with and make it even better."

I treasured the dialogues those visits triggered, but all the while my list of potential artists got smaller and smaller. Some of the artists felt this work would be too stressful. Some were concerned that the commission would require them to invent a whole new mode of working. Still others questioned whether they could survive the three to four or more years that they projected would be required for the commission. Even so, every sculptor was wholly supportive of and excited by the concept. Over and over they reminded me that

no integration of sculpture and architecture of this scope, scale, and impact had been attempted for hundreds of years.

IT PROVIDED ONE OF THE GREAT ARTISTIC OPPORTUNITIES OF THE CENTURY.

As the interviews progressed, I became more and more aware that it would not be possible for any one sculptor to carry out this important and complex commission. In fact, I decided that the project would benefit in interest, in creativity, and in diversity by allowing several artists to contribute their visions within the established framework. I was deeply moved by this idea of multiple sculptors to create multiple sculptures. The rightness of this decision resonated with my growing sense that the Memorial needed this broader visual vocabulary.

In my final recommendation to the FDR Memorial Commission, I proposed four nationally recognized sculptors for this great task. I suggested that each would be assigned one or two locations, and that the work of each would be integrated into the whole scheme. I felt that the assignment of specific themes for the sculptors would grow out of their individual strengths, and I proposed a sculpture workshop based on a method I had been evolving for years. This method, which I call *Taking Part,* is designed to foster creativity and reach consensus.

Collaboration and Development

The Taking Part Workshop that I proposed for the artists was an exciting prospect. I had used this technique to generate creativity within my own office, to facilitate mutual agreement in professional collaborations, and to allow citizens to participate in the design of their own communities. But bringing together a superstar group of artists in an intense collaboration within an already established architectural framework offered new and exciting challenges.

The commission considered all of my recommendations and added some of their own. The list of four sculptors was finalized:

Leonard Baskin,
Neil Estern,
Robert Graham and
George Segal.

(At a later date, Tom Hardy was selected to undertake the addition of FDR's unique presidential seal of the United States as an entry piece for the Memorial.)

The four sculptors did not know each other. They were not in the habit of working collaboratively in the way that architects and landscape architects commonly join together professionally.
They were unused to the idea of fusing their creativity with other artists. It was a daunting task!
I explained my Taking Part Workshop process and how I had developed it over time as a working methodology. George Segal, as always very articulate, spoke for the whole group when he said:
"It sounds damned interesting. Your design will provide a stabilizing influence and it makes perfect sense—but of course every one of us is trained to stubborn individualism. The process sounds both pragmatic and idealistic. I'll say yes."

So we planned for this first artistic jam session and met together in early November 1977, in San Francisco. In preparation, we had much to do. Each artist had received architectural plans and sketches, but I soon realized they were unaccustomed to interpreting architectural drawings.
Although we had a model of the basic site plan of the Memorial, I was concerned about their grasp of the scale of things, so we leased a large warehouse and built an eighty-foot-long model. Then we rented garage dollies, like those used to slide underneath cars. The idea was that the artists could lie down and move through the site model at eye level—and thereby get a feeling for the real scale of the proposed Memorial.

Artists interact with a large-scale model in order to better understand the scale of the Memorial.

24

The first meeting of the sculpture group includes (from left) Wanda Hanson, Lawrence Halprin, Leonard Baskin, Bob Graham, Sue Yung Li Ikeda, Neil Estern, and Tom Aidala.

We spent four very intense days together. I believe we were all nervous and concerned about the outcome. The first day's meeting was tense. Leonard Baskin, when introduced to George Segal, said, "I never thought to become a friend of a pop artist." George just smiled. Speaking to me about it a year later, Leonard reminisced, "I attacked Segal at the beginning, but he turned my vituperation aside and answered like the angel he is."

We got through that first day and carried on. We talked about our personal memories of FDR and how he had affected us. We talked about historically important moments and events from the era. My staff had developed an image bank with photographs of Franklin Delano Roosevelt at all stages of his life. We pinned these images on the walls and discussed them, hoping to find mutual agreements as to which images we might want to use. We considered sculptural clusters, we developed themes, and we produced a general storyboard for the Memorial.

It became clear to us that sculptures which depicted only FDR could not carry the vitality of what happened during those years.

The drama of the times required references to the events and the people who were affected by them.

These two panels are part of the image bank that was used as a resource for the sculpture workshop.

These images, interacting with the words of FDR, could evoke an enormously powerful response to the unfolding story. This approach had the potential of humanizing earth-shattering events which had changed the course of history.

This approach also suited the character of FDR and his constant respect for and interaction with ordinary people. My most powerful memory of him is from the newsreels of the day. They captured FDR driving about in his convertible, meeting with his public, and finding out first-hand about their fears and hopes for the future. I was sad that for budgetary reasons we had lost a proposed interpretive center where these newsreels could have been viewed.

George Segal prepares
an early clay maquette as
Halprin looks on.

After working so closely together, we pulled apart for a
while, and each sculptor then worked by himself
searching for ideas from the image bank which he
might use. Then, together again, we attacked the entire
Memorial in a frenzy of collective energy and
collaboration. This format of individual work sessions
interspersed with group collaborations continued for
several days, until we arrived at an agreement about the
content and the images to be developed to express this
content. Perhaps the most interesting outcome—besides the camaraderie—was the ease with
which these decisions were reached. When we finally discussed who would develop each image and
where it should be located, there was no division of opinion. Each artist agreed to take on specific
tasks in specific locations and the others concurred. It was remarkable! George Segal quipped:
"I'm not used to all this help in being creative."

The result of the workshop was that we decided on the basic themes.

The *first-term* room would concentrate on the
FIRST 100 DAYS OF FDR'S PRESIDENCY.
It would be symbolized by an image which recalled
FDR's inauguration in 1933.

The *second-term* room would deal with the social
issues of the day—the GREAT DEPRESSION and
UNEMPLOYMENT. The problems would be
exemplified by a cluster of images depicting a farm
couple, an urban breadline, and a "Fireside Chat."
The solutions to the problems would be presented by
a mural depicting FDR's social programs.

The *third-term* room would concentrate on
WORLD WAR II. We assumed that there would be
an image of FDR as commander in chief.

The *fourth-term* room would be devoted to
PEACE and there would be a strong reference to the
United Nations. It was also decided that the fourth-
term room should deal specifically with FDR's death.
That would be portrayed by a bas-relief of his funeral
cortege. Soon after the peace treaties were signed and
early in his fourth term, President Franklin Delano
Roosevelt died. As in the biblical story of Moses, who
led his people to the promised land but was never able
to cross into it, FDR brought his country through
the trials and tribulations of a devastating war but was
not able to enjoy the peace.

In the year that followed this workshop, each sculptor carried his assignment forward. In order to present their basic intentions to one another, to the FDR Memorial Commission, and to the Commission of Fine Arts, they developed maquettes, which are similar to sculptural sketches, of their proposals. By January 1978, it was time for a second jam session. This was held in George Segal's studio in New Jersey. It was bitter cold, and we were all shivering and anxious to share our progress.

The Second World War

After reviewing our various maquettes, we turned our attention to an issue which had stymied us during the first workshop.

How were we going to deal with World War II?

We had struggled with this issue and left the first session feeling frustrated, uneasy, and unresolved on that count. None of our sculptural concepts for WWII had satisfied us. We took it up again on the second day of the second session. The war was perhaps the most significant event of all our lifetimes. It had cost the world millions of lives, and it had dominated five years that all of us had experienced. We remembered the satisfaction of feeling the rightness of fighting a war that had preserved the ideals upon which our country had been founded. The resolution of this issue was probably the most important thing to come out of the second jam session.

We recognized that eventually other memorials would be built that would speak of specific wars. Their emphasis would inevitably be about their own battles and their own dead. This has already happened with the Vietnam and the Korean Wars, and planning has begun for the World War II Memorial.

We theorized that in those war memorials the primary emphasis would be on the specific battles, the specific losses. In our situation, the FDR Memorial had to deal with many social events, as well as the war and the peace that followed. We felt that we should not overemphasize the battle aspects of the war at the expense of all the other vital social issues of the Roosevelt era. With this in mind, we decided to take our direction from President Roosevelt's own words about war.

In an address at Chautauqua, New York, on August 14, 1936, he said,

"I have seen war. I have seen war on land and sea. I have seen blood running from the wounded... I have seen the dead in the mud. I have seen cities destroyed... I have seen children starving. I have seen the agony of mothers and wives. I hate war."

Leonard Baskin (left) and Halprin study the first War Wall model.

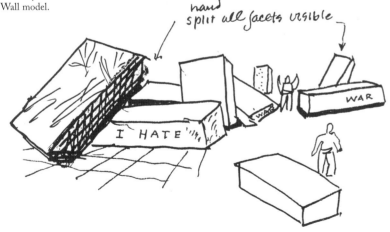

split all facets visible

hand

WAR

I HATE

The war wall.

As we talked about the war, President Roosevelt's thoughts on war, and our personal experiences with war, we grew emotional. We talked louder and shuffled about in the cold studio, frustrated. Some of us waved our arms around violently. The stone model we were working with was knocked down on the table. Suddenly we all realized we had captured the destructive image that expressed what we needed. We immediately began referring to it as the War Wall and determined that President Roosevelt's "I hate war" quotation would be carved behind it. Leonard Baskin later said: "The most incredible thing which occurred during this second collaboration grew out of Halprin's dissatisfaction and all our frustration. I don't know if he could have arrived at the broken wall solution by himself. It was the result of our collaborative anger and frustration."

This proved to be a great catharsis for all of us, and we were able to break through this impasse and move forward. We discussed the appropriateness of the War Wall and how it would describe by implication the devastation of war—broken lands, broken cities, broken people. We considered adding sculptures within the rubble but finally decided that FDR's quote was enough. We decided, too, that FDR's refrain, "I hate war," would be repeated in the fallen stone rubble.

Our next area of discussion was how to emphasize the enormous thrust toward peace that grew stronger and more determined as the war drew to a close. As a group, we had developed a growing concern about celebrating Eleanor Roosevelt's contribution to FDR's presidency and the impact she had on the country. Every historian, every book about this period has emphasized her importance and the influence she had on the president through her interest in social programs, concern for children and the downtrodden, worry for the welfare of our soldiers, and deep determination to facilitate the emerging peace. In my early presentations of the Memorial concept, the FDR Memorial Commission had been negative about including Mrs. Roosevelt. "Franklin Delano Roosevelt was elected president," they said, "not his wife."

An early clay maquette of Eleanor Roosevelt stands in Neil Estern's Brooklyn studio.

The issue was kept alive, however, and when we finally suggested that Mrs. Roosevelt be included in her capacities as our first delegate to the United Nations, the commission enthusiastically agreed. She would be seen standing in front of the seal of the United Nations in the fourth-term room of the Memorial.

The major role of the series of Taking Part Workshops was to provide a vehicle for the artists to work together, each drawing upon their own strengths and focusing their efforts on their own styles. This approach allowed us to create an integrated single work of art. From this point on, the Memorial could be seen as an artistic whole.

Words on stone

During the year the artists had worked to develop their maquettes, I searched for a stone carver and the proper letter design for the FDR inscriptions.

John Benson, who had been highly recommended by Leonard Baskin, had joined our team at the second artist's workshop. The important linkage between the sculpture and FDR's quotations had become more and more evident, and we believed it needed to be considered as part of the whole artistic concept.

John Benson carves his first demonstration inscription into a Carnelian granite sample.

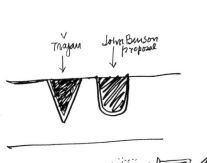

John Benson proposed a letter design for the Memorial, a classic Trajan style with elegant and formal letters. He carved a test on a great slab of the Carnelian granite and demonstrated how he could integrate his carving into a granite surface that was sometimes heavily pillowed. The FDR Commission liked this style, and at the workshop John was prepared to continue his paper layouts as the quotations were chosen. But as we reviewed full-scale layouts of more and more quotations, a simpler sans serif letterform evolved. This new letter is unique to the Memorial and is more related to the letterforms of the New Deal era.

And so, during the workshop, we began to synchronize the content and location of sculptures and quotations. We talked about our choice of quotes and the length and layout of the carvings. All of us were excited and full of opinions about what quotations should accompany the artwork in the context of the overall themes of each room. In the first room, we knew we wanted to reference President Roosevelt's famous admonition, "The only thing we have to fear is fear itself." We knew that this statement, which changed the whole mood of the country, would have to appear as a large headline above the sculptural image *First Inaugural*.

We imagined the quotes that would accompany and underscore the images of the Great Depression and the war years. FDR's words were poignant and powerful and evocative. These quotations were necessary as part of the history lesson. Some would interact with the art and others would stand on their own.

Although I had lived through the Roosevelt years and the resonance of his words still reverberated in my mind, I felt the need to augment the quotations we had selected. I turned to Dr. William Luchtenburg, a renowned FDR scholar, for discussions about FDR's most important achievements and about the quotations that would best express them. Dr. Luchtenburg was immensely helpful in his suggestions and his evaluations. In addition, I presented my recommendations to the FDR Memorial Commission, and they too suggested some additional quotations. It was at that time also that the commission suggested that we include a sculpture of FDR's dog Fala and his personal presidential seal as part of the Memorial. While the sculptors and stone carver were working back in their studios, my attention turned to other major elements in the Memorial. With the storyboard for the walking experience established, I thought of how the wall would act as a backdrop for the artists' images.

Halprin explains the placement of individual stones using clay models of the granite wall.

I thought of the wall in musical terms
and studied the elevations
in model form as if they were made up
of notes on a page.

The stones contained many properties—length, shape, depth (protrusions and recesses), smoothness, roughness. These qualities allowed for almost infinite variety and variation. Keeping these factors in mind, I was able to visualize in the same way that a composer documents his musical arrangements: I wrote "scores" of stony relationship that I could see in my mind's eye as I mentally walked through the Memorial.

Where the wall extended from the entrance, I knew that it should start shifting its texture and character. The first section of the stone, at the small entrance building, needed to present a simple, smooth character. That smooth finish would continue throughout the outdoor rooms which represent the first and second terms of FDR's presidency. As visitors approached the third-term room, with the advent of the war, the wall needed to become more agitated. That roughness would continue until the wall reached the niche which housed the sculpture *Funeral Cortege*. At that point the wall would become more subdued. In the fourth-term room, however, the stone again grows rugged and exuberant. In this room, the large-scale expansiveness would express optimism and joy. The war had ended, and there was hope for world unity and peace.

Water

It was also time for me to revisit the design of the water elements in the Memorial—the fountains. These fountains would fall from the granite walls. They needed to be carefully integrated into the pattern of the stones and the sculptures. Water was a major component in the plan.

FDR poses aboard the *Vireo* with his sons James and Elliot at Campobello Island, New Brunswick, Canada, August 1920.

The guidelines I had received from the FDR Memorial Commission had pointed out how significant water had been in Roosevelt's life. It had been a constant leitmotif. His family had come from sea captains in the China trade, and FDR was born and raised at the edge of the Hudson River. He had wanted to go to the naval academy at Annapolis, instead, he ended up at Harvard, where the Charles River was a significant element of the landscape. FDR was an avid sailor. And in his early political career, he was assistant secretary of the navy.

FDR and other patients
receive therapy at
Warm Springs, Georgia,
circa 1930.

Water, of course, was also related to FDR's polio. In 1921, FDR fell ill at the family's summer home in Campobello after a day's swimming with his sons in the frigid water of the Atlantic. Although the water did not cause FDR's poliomyelitis, he must have associated the chilly ocean with the event, because, while developing a therapeutic treatment center for polio at Warm Springs, Georgia, he said,

"The water put me where I am, and the water has to put me back."

Later as president, FDR spent much time on board the *Potomac*, the presidential yacht he had converted from a coast guard cutter. The president loved ships, he loved destroyers, and he loved to take the helm. Many significant meetings with Churchill were held shipboard during the war years.

The water in the Memorial speaks about life's basic issues—water represents nature, health, power, and agricultural plenty. All life forms grew from and are dependent upon water.

Water propelled early migrations, adventures, and explorations. Water brings animation to urban centers through sound, light reflections, and cooling spray. Water brings all these associations to the FDR Memorial, whether or not they are perceived consciously.

Quite aside from the commission's interest and my own leanings toward the use of water, however, I soon realized that it would be a functionally important element in the Memorial as well. National Airport, a major facility for Washington, D.C., travelers, is located just a short distance across the river from the Memorial site. During early site visits I experienced the impact these take-offs and landings would have on the Memorial ambiance. I often clocked the planes passing over the site at one-minute intervals, sometimes less.

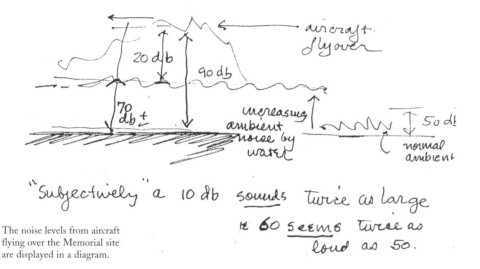

The noise levels from aircraft flying over the Memorial site are displayed in a diagram.

The sound was powerful and distracting, and it tested at over ninety decibels while the planes were overhead. Normal ambient noise at the site was fifty decibels. We felt that any reduction of the flyover noise would be extremely helpful to the overall enjoyment of the Memorial.

Water, especially if it is moving and splashing, creates its own ambient sound, and I had found it extremely effective in masking unwanted traffic and construction noise in projects in cities. I felt enthusiastic about linking the masking ability of the sound of water with the symbolic use of water as a design element that recalled President Roosevelt's own involvement with water.

This joining of design symbolism and functional benefit led to the inclusion of active waterfalls in each of the four rooms. In each space the character of the waterfall is different, reflecting in its own specific concept unique historical moments during FDR's presidency. In the second-term room, for example, the layered fountain reflects the character of dams in the Tennessee Valley Authority, one of the agencies formed by FDR.

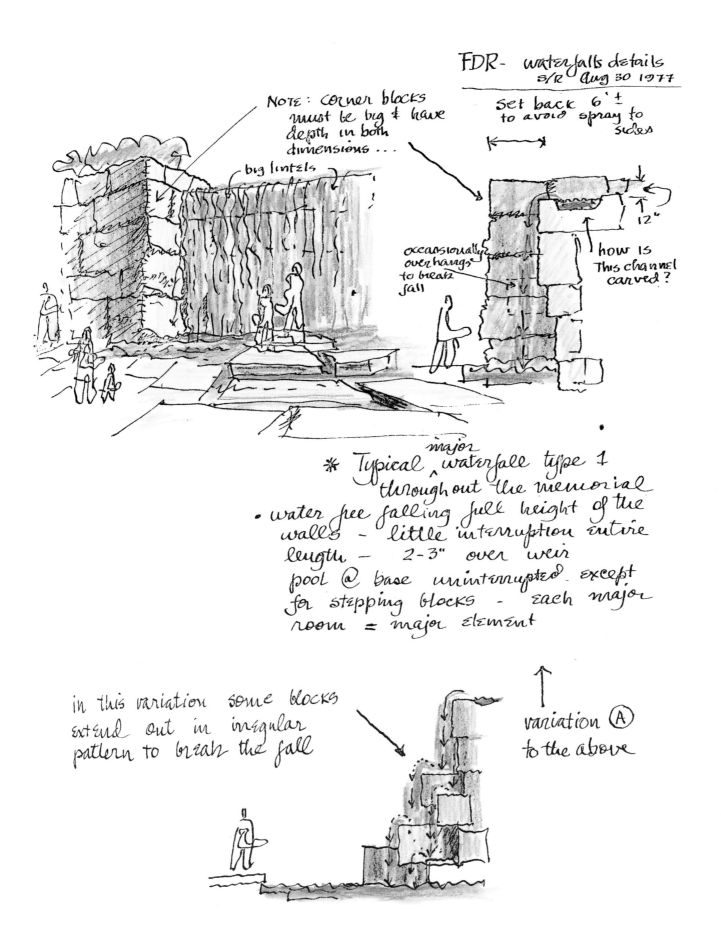

FDR- waterfalls details
s/r Aug 30 1977

NOTE: corner blocks must be big & have depth in both dimensions ...

big lintels

Set back 6' ± to avoid spray to sides

12"

occasionally overhangs to break fall

how is this channel carved?

* Typical major waterfall type 1 throughout the memorial
• water free falling full height of the walls - little interruption entire length - 2-3" over weir pool @ base uninterrupted except for stepping blocks - each major room = major element

in this variation some blocks extend out in irregular pattern to break the fall

variation Ⓐ to the above

35

Plantings

The final element to be integrated into the Memorial was the planting. Basic protection of existing trees—the 100-foot-high elms and the Japanese cherry trees—had been considered early on in designing the overall layout of the site. Now it was time to consider how to best complement President Roosevelt's interests and the story of the Memorial through plant materials.

FDR loved trees and was deeply interested in conservation, forestry, and reforestation. He spoke of his intention to retire to a forestry practice at his home in Hyde Park, New York, after his presidency. He considered himself a country man and often called himself a farmer. I needed to take this information into consideration.

None of the existing trees on the peninsula were native to the site. The dominant trees were the elms, which had been planted after the Army Corps of Engineers had "built" the peninsula while dredging the Tidal Basin. These trees stood along a road bordering the basin. Some of the trees, however, had become infected by Dutch elm disease, and I was concerned that they would not survive for very long. The elms were accompanied by groupings of holly trees, which added an evergreen quality to the site. They would be important during the winter months. Then there were the Japanese cherries, a gift from the people of Japan, which had been planted in 1912. Except for a few exotic additions, such as several hemlocks and a pawlonia, there were no other plantings. The Memorial needed groundcovers, color in the gardenlike passageways, a backdrop on the slopes behind the granite wall, and trees for shade.

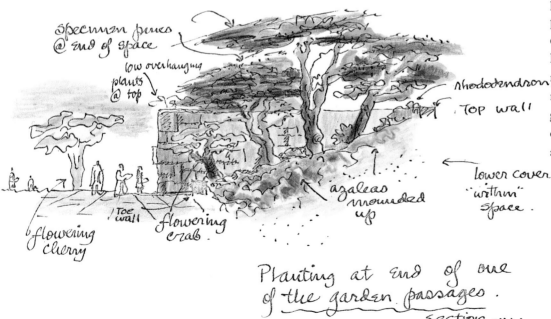

specimen pines @ end of space

low overhanging plants @ top

rhododendron

Top wall

flowering cherry

Toe wall

flowering crab

azaleas mounded up

lower cover "within" space.

Planting at end of one of the garden passages.

section....

Locations on the site..
There will be a need to protect trees & plants that must be saved during the construction phase -- I suppose the playing fields areas will have to be closed as a corporation yard !!

Within the memorial area flowering trees:— many on slopes & along the lower wall in the garden passages: ————

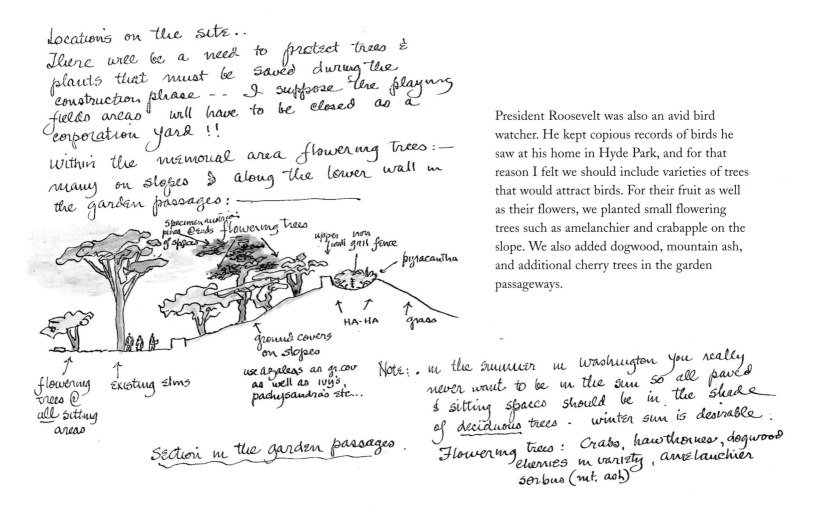

Specimen austrian pine @ ends of slope
flowering trees
upper iron wall grill fence
pyracantha
ground covers on slopes
HA-HA
grass
flowering trees @ all sitting areas
Existing elms
use azaleas as gr.cov as well as ivy's, pachysandra's etc...

Section in the garden passages.

Note:. in the summer in Washington you really never want to be in the sun so all paved & sitting spaces should be in the shade of deciduous trees - winter sun is desirable.
Flowering trees: Crabs, hawthornes, dogwood cherries in variety, amelanchier sorbus (mt. ash)

President Roosevelt was also an avid bird watcher. He kept copious records of birds he saw at his home in Hyde Park, and for that reason I felt we should include varieties of trees that would attract birds. For their fruit as well as their flowers, we planted small flowering trees such as amelanchier and crabapple on the slope. We also added dogwood, mountain ash, and additional cherry trees in the garden passageways.

In the woodland planting behind the walls as well as throughout the Memorial, I sought out a variety of forestlike trees, rather than employing the usual type of single-purpose monoculture usually used as a formal architectural framework.

I was particularly interested in finding species that would provide color during the autumn months as well as using pine to lend an evergreen feeling in winter.

Trees, shrubs, and groundcovers were then located on the plan in relationship to the walls, artwork, sightlines, quotations, and fountains. The overall ambiance and the emotional impact of specific sculptural vignettes and contemplative passageways were considered.

The plantings had to be sensitive to and reflect the complexity of the Memorial.

Breaking Ground

The first construction work for the Memorial began in October 1994. We knew that the Lincoln and Jefferson Memorials had continuing problems with settlement, so we had tested the bearing capacity of the filled ground which made up our site. The peninsula had been built up in the late part of the nineteenth century with mud dredged from the bottom of the Tidal Basin, and tests showed that, in spite of 100 years of natural settlement, it would not support our proposed construction. In order to minimize cracking and settlement of the FDR Memorial, our first task was to drive 900 pilings down to solid ground, approximately eighty to 100 feet.

The tops of steel pilings that will support the Memorial are seen here during the first winter of construction.

In room four, the granite blocks are hoisted into position.

Concrete grade beams were then built over the pilings to form a reinforced concrete deck which would support our construction. Essentially, the Memorial was being built on a bridge.

During all the months of construction, we continued our trips to the quarry. Special stones were selected, shapes and forms of manufactured stones were monitored, and mock-ups of each type of wall construction were reviewed and approved. Samples of various construction styles were tested and refined. The craftsmanship of the quarry workers at Cold Spring was superb and it remained so under some very trying conditions. When I visited the quarry during severe winter months, when temperatures often dropped below zero, they brought out a special transportable warming hut for me.

Also during the construction period I made special trips to tree farms and plant nurseries to select specimens of the various trees and shrubs we had chosen. The large trees needed special treatment if they were to be relocated successfully—they had to be root-pruned, balled, burlapped, fed, and acclimatized, so that the shock of moving would be minimized. The project benefited from this early selection process: the specimens had two years of growth before planting and the success rate of the transplants was improved.

At the Halka nursery, a tree specimen is dug, balled, and burlapped.

After much of the stone had been installed on the walls and the spaces became more defined, I started to plant the large trees within the core of the Memorial. The effect was electrifying. The large trees set up a new and fascinating veil-like series of planes in front of the walls. Pine branches swung down across the granite, softening its hard contours. In the rooms, the trees established a new, heightened sense of scale which seemed to double and triple the size of the twelve-foot-high walls. The granite skyline which had dominated the vertical height of the Memorial in an almost continuous line, was now pierced by a series of arching trees— of maple, zelkova, and locust. Whereas the granite was impenetrable, the green of the trees and the spread of their branchlets created a lacy, antimacassar-like network on the skyline.

As visitors walk through the Memorial, I hope that they will in some measure relive the twelve years of FDR's presidency. I hope that the sculptural vignettes give life to their understanding of that time, and I hope that they will almost hear FDR's voice. During the difficult days of the Great Depression and later during the frightening, painful days of World War II, President Roosevelt's speeches, exhortations, and "Fireside Chats" exuded optimism and engendered action. His words were invigorating, ennobling, and motivating. He lifted the spirits of the entire country, he gave us courage, and he showed us the way. This Memorial seeks to evoke those times as well as that man.

A Japanese white pine has been planted to frame the fountain in the fourth-term room.

AS VISITORS APPROACH THE FDR MEMORIAL, they should cast their minds back in time to the early 1930s. Imagine an America before televisions and computers, an America that was not completely dependent on cars, an America that still relied heavily on family farms. The country had recently suffered a devastating stock market crash; in panic, people rushed to withdraw their life's savings, but the banks could not pay them. Banks were foreclosing on home and farm loans, jobs were evaporating, and cities as well as small towns were filled with the unemployed. The country was in the Great Depression. There were no social safety nets; each person was on his own, and the role of government was quite different than it is today.

In the dark Depression of October 1932, when FDR was first running for office, the musical *Americana* made its appearance at the Shubert Theatre in New York City. The spirit of the times was embodied in the lyrics of one of the songs from that musical: "Brother, Can You Spare a Dime?"

Depositors rush to withdraw their savings from the People's Trust & Savings, Chicago, Illinois, June 1932.

A farmer plows his field with the help of a mule in Gee's Bend, Alabama, 1937. This photograph was taken by Arthur Rothstein as part of the Resettlement Administration.

This study model shows the
entrance to the Memorial.

Conjuring up these images would be a good preparation for visitors as they approach the small
entrance plaza for the Memorial. This forecourt, shaded by zelkova trees, forms an outdoor
lobby which offers an opportunity to stop and get oriented.

THE PLAZA IS A PLACE OF ANTICIPATION.

The east side of the forecourt lobby is
defined by a small stone building
which houses park ranger offices and a
small bookstore and interpretive area.
Visitors can see photos of President
Roosevelt here, as well as look
through books and ask questions of
the rangers.

The ceremonial entrance to the
Memorial lies straight ahead and is
announced by a twelve-foot-high granite
wall, which heralds the beginning of
the Memorial experience with the
words: "Franklin Delano Roosevelt,
President of the United States,
1933–1945."

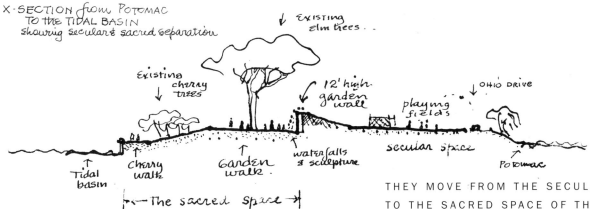

X·SECTION from POTOMAC
TO the TIDAL BASIN
showing secular & sacred separation

↓ EXISTING
elm trees ··

Existing
cherry
trees ↓

12' high
garden
wall ↓

↓ OHIO DRIVE

playing
fields

secular space

↑
Tidal
basin

Cherry
walk

↑
Garden
walk.

waterfalls
& sculpture

POTOMAC

←·— The sacred space —→

The visitor has arrived, but, in order to enter, he or she must negotiate a medieval-style gateway that recalls the early entrances to ancient stone-walled cities. This transitional space symbolically cues visitors to shed their everyday concerns and honor the Memorial experience.

THEY MOVE FROM THE SECULAR SPACE OF THE OUTSIDE WORLD TO THE SACRED SPACE OF THE MEMORIAL.

The Memorial will unfold from this point like a processional narrative. The vehicle for the story is the stone wall. Carved inscriptions, bronze sculptures, and waterfalls emanate from the walls and convey the events of an era.

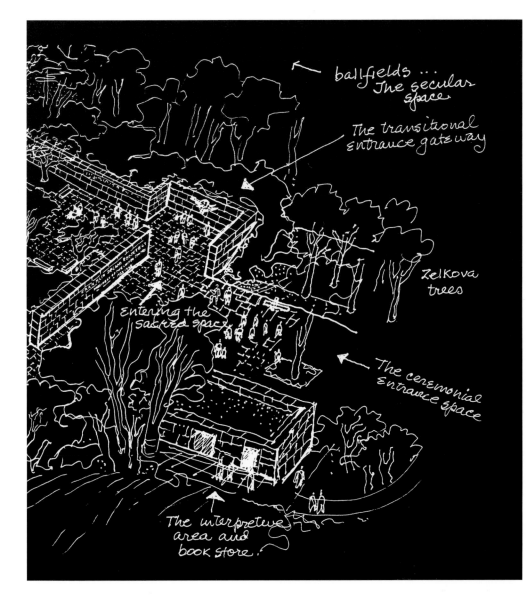

ballfields …
The secular
space.

The transitional
entrance gateway

Zelkova
trees

Entering the
sacred space

The ceremonial
entrance space

The interpretive
area and
book store.

The First Term
1933–1937

The stone in this first-term room has a simple split-face finish and is similar in feel to the New England fieldstone used at FDR's homes in Hyde Park, New York. Memorable quotations from FDR's speeches and "Fireside Chats" have been carved in large letters directly on the granite, while longer quotations are sandblasted in smaller letters on thermal-finished granite panels.

FDR's presidential years start here. The primary theme of this room is the immediate impact that his tremendous energy and optimism had on the country, from the day he took his first oath of office.

As visitors step forward into the gateway space, they are met by the bronze sculpture *Presidential Seal* which was inspired by the seal that President Roosevelt used throughout his twelve years in office. It can be seen in the photograph of his first inauguration. This seal has unique characteristics—there is no shield over the eagle's body, there are no arrows or olive branches grasped in the eagle's claws, and there are 48 stars.

The artistic rendition of the presidential seal for the Memorial is by Tom Hardy of Portland, Oregon, who specializes in sculpting animal and bird figures. He built this sculpture by painstakingly cutting small pieces from bronze plates and welding them together, with careful attention to all the intricate detail of the American bald eagle. This technique is unique within the Memorial, for all of the other sculptures are cast in bronze.

Studies by Tom Hardy for his sculpture of the *Presidential Seal.*

THIS GENERATION OF

FDR is inaugurated as the thirty-second president of the United States on March 4, 1933.

On the wall to the left of the *Presidential Seal* is a line from one of FDR's most famous speeches during his first term. In an address to the American public on June 27, 1936, FDR spoke with full knowledge and understanding of the challenges the country still faced. He called upon all Americans to accept the tasks of their time with these words:

"THERE IS A MYSTERIOUS CYCLE IN HUMAN EVENTS.
TO SOME GENERATIONS MUCH IS GIVEN.
OF OTHER GENERATIONS MUCH IS EXPECTED.

AMERICANS HAS A RENDEZVOUS WITH DESTINY."

With these words, the president both acknowledged the difficult times the country was going through and proclaimed the confidence he had that we would be able to cope with and overcome them.

This still is taken from a movie by Glenn Fleck, which was used to explain the concept of the Memorial to the Congress and the FDR Memorial Commission. This view of the Washington Monument is now seen from room one.

As visitors turn into the first-term room, there is a magnificent view across the Tidal Basin to the Washington Monument, the obelisk around which the Lincoln, Jefferson and Roosevelt Memorials visually pivot. Symbolically, the Washington Monument articulates the centrality and the importance of our commitment to the results of the Washington era—the Constitution, the Declaration of Independence, and democracy.

The other three presidential memorials speak to our country's reactions to various challenges to that commitment. Those who are drawn to this view may wish to walk eastward, down to the Tidal Basin to sit on a bench and look outward to the view. Afterwards, they can return to the passageway between rooms one and two and continue the procession.

The quotations in this first room define Roosevelt's platform for moving forward and galvanizing our resolve as a country. At a time when twelve million people were out of work and millions had lost their savings, people needed an optimistic and energetic leader to rally their spirits and encourage their efforts.

FDR's words, delivered with his youthful confidence, his quick wit, and his open sympathy for the plight of those in need, provided the country with a healing tonic.

Election night crowds in New York's Times Square spontaneously sang "Happy Days Are Here Again" when it became obvious that Franklin Delano Roosevelt would be their next president.

On the campaign trail in California, FDR stands alongside (from left) son James, Senator William McAdoo, and advisor James Farley as he is introduced by Will Rogers. 1932.

The famous entertainer-philosopher Will Rogers said it well on March 5, 1933, one day after FDR took office. "Americans haven't been as happy in three years as they are today. No money, no banks, no work, no nothing, but they know they got a man in there who is wise to Congress, wise to our so-called big men. The whole country is with him, just so he does something. If he burned down the capital, we would cheer and say, 'Well, we at least got a fire started anyhow.'"

FDR, with Eleanor (left) and son James (right), departs in a triumphant mood, after voting in the 1932 election.

President Roosevelt's ebullient personality and style were important elements in the fight to lift the emotional depression which gripped the country. This aspect of the president is captured in the sculpture *First Inaugural*. It expresses Roosevelt's delight at being president and at having the opportunity to serve his country. This bas-relief also reveals the relationship FDR had with the American people. In the background of the motorcade, crowds of supporters line the streets as he passes. They strain to get a glimpse of the new president in whom they have invested their hopes for the future. The president responds to their thunderous cheers with his usual self-confidence and spontaneously waves his top hat. His smiling, expressive face is full of vitality. All this is in direct contrast to the feelings of the previous administration, whose president, Herbert Hoover, had implied that the country was at the end of its strength and there was nothing more we could do.

President Herbert Hoover and the president-elect ride together to FDR's first inauguration on March 4, 1933.

Sculptor ROBERT GRAHAM captured all of FDR's exuberant characteristics in a bronze bas-relief that exudes optimism. The image is based on newsreel coverage, for that was the medium through which most people saw FDR.

The sculptor selected a moment from the frames of the newsreel of FDR's first inauguration. He has emphasized the movement of the car passing the cheering crowds by sculpting a background that is slightly out of focus and has lines running through it. The figure of the president, however, is in focus, as though to emphasize his strength and his importance at this critical point in history.

Robert Graham is a figurative sculptor with an uncanny facility for capturing the evocative spirit of the person he is portraying. In this way he carries his sculpture beyond mere portraiture to the realm of universal symbolism.

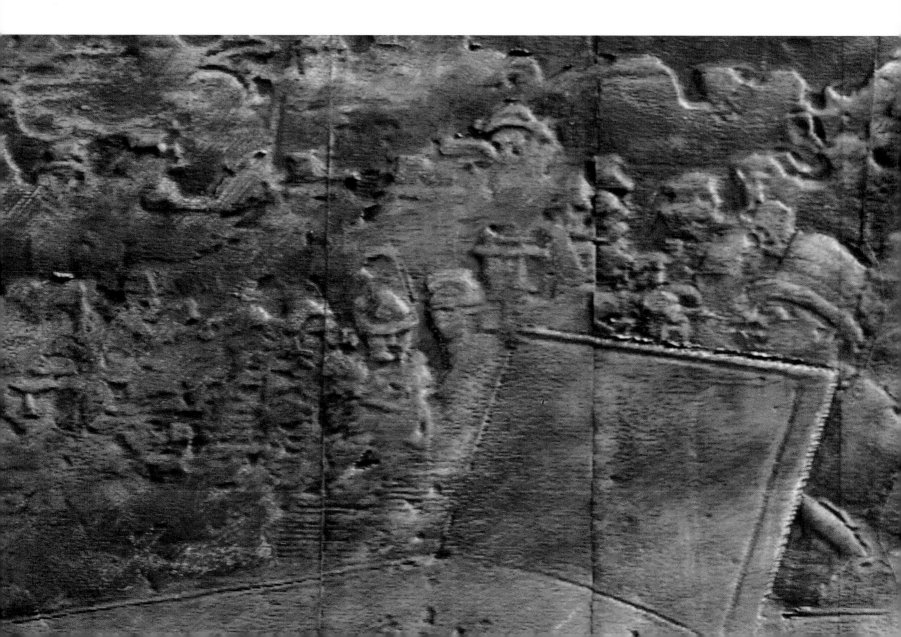

Like FDR's simple and direct message regarding justice for all,
the waterfall in this first room is simple and direct in its design.

It speaks of the type of water one encounters in the New England countryside where FDR began
his journey toward the presidency. It also reminds us of FDR's deep love for and understanding of
the basic elements of nature. As visitors experience this first-term room they will encounter
another FDR quote which deals with this concern. On January 24, 1935, he wrote a message
to the Congress regarding the abuse of our natural resources, which had recently resulted in
floods and dust storms. It was an innovative theme that foretold our nation's growing concern for
the preservation of our environment.

"MEN AND NATURE MUST WORK HAND IN HAND.
THE THROWING OUT OF BALANCE OF THE
RESOURCES OF NATURE THROWS OUT OF BALANCE
ALSO THE LIVES OF MEN."

As visitors leave the first-term room and continue the processional into the passageway which leads to room two, the parklike aspect of the Memorial's character takes over. Nature and plantings predominate here. This is an opportunity for visitors to relax and contemplate.

The quality of the experience shifts to a calm and meditative mood similar to that experienced in a garden. This aspect of the Memorial encourages sitting, reflection, and enjoyment of a serene space with an intimate, peaceful feeling. To the east, there are holly and cherry trees which block longer views across the Tidal Basin. To the west, a sloping lawn rises up to the height of the granite walls.

The backdrop for this tranquil passageway is an arch of azalea, rhododendron, viburnum and other spring blooming shrubs, topped by a low cluster of dogwood and crabapple and a taller planting of deciduous canopy trees such as sugar maple, liquid amber, and pin oak. High on the slope toward the end of the passageway, there is a dense green clump of pines that visually contains the space.

At the end of the passageway, visitors encounter a fountain that serves as a transitional marker. The scale of the fountain is small and fits with the character of the passageway. The water emerges from the granite wall, passes through a granite basin, and falls into a pool below. The scale and sound are appropriate to this more private space, but they also prepare visitors for their entry back into the public flow of the Memorial.

Shadows of the plantings in passageway one interplay with this archetypal, stony fountain.

The end of the passageway marks the beginning of FDR's second term in office. The next outdoor room will portray the continuing impact of the Depression and FDR's efforts to overcome the social problems that resulted from it.

As seen from atop a 100-foot
water tower, a dust storm
blows through Kansas.

AS THE DEPRESSION DEEPENED, natural disasters added to economic disasters. Rexford Tugwell, in his book *FDR: Architect of an Era*, graphically described the situation: "In 1934 and 1936 the prairies beyond the Mississippi simply dried up. There was little winter snow to feed underground springs; in the summer the sun burned up the vegetation, leaving the land bare. Starving cattle and sheep ate the grasses down to the roots; and when the winds came the dust blew up in clouds until the air was thick. It drifted against the fences and left the subsoil exposed where crops had once grown. The droughts came to a country that never should have been broken to the plow….From a green beginning, in the spring of 1934, the country beyond the Mississippi, especially western Kansas, Nebraska, and the Dakotas, had a complete crop failure in the months that followed. Then eastern Colorado, Oklahoma, and Texas began to show signs of blowing. The southern areas began to be called 'the dust bowl.'"

Tugwell went on to translate these natural crises into human terms: "At one time three-fourths of families in the dust bowl were getting government help. It was more than a local disaster; it was a national problem. The president had diverted as much of his emergency funds as he could to relieve this area, and the struggle with nature was watched by an entire nation."

These are your tan-faced children.

These skilled men, idle, with holes in their shoes.

These drifters from State to State, these wolvish, bewildered boys

Who ride the blinds and the box-cars from jail to jail,

Burnt in their youth like cinders of hot smokestacks,

Learning the thief's crouch and the cadger's whine,

Dishonored, abandoned, disinherited.

These, dying in the bright sunlight they cannot eat,

Or the strong men, sitting at home, their hands clasping nothing,

looking at their lost hands.

These are your tan-faced children, the parched young,

The old man rooting in waste-heaps, the family rotting

In the flat, before eviction,

With the toys of plenty about them,

The shiny toys making ice and music and light,

But no price for the shiny toys and the last can empty.

The sleepers in blind corners of the night. "I SEE ONE-THIRD OF

The women with dry breasts and phantom eyes.

The walkers upon nothing, the four million.

These are your tan-faced children.

Ode to Walt Whitman
Stephen Vincent Benet, 1936

A destitute family ekes out a living from a wooden shack in Arkansas.

A NATION ILL-HOUSED, ILL-CLAD, ILL-NOURISHED.

THE TEST OF OUR PROGRESS IS NOT WHETHER WE ADD MORE TO THE ABUNDANCE OF THOSE WHO HAVE MUCH; IT IS WHETHER WE PROVIDE ENOUGH FOR THOSE WHO HAVE TOO LITTLE."

Second Inaugural Address
January 20, 1937

subway stations. In the country people
lost their farms and ranches. They
were uprooted from their communities
and formed a vast population of
migrants. Pushing their meager
possessions in barrows or loading their
families into beat-up cars and trucks,
they struck out across the country
looking for work.

On January 9, 1940, in a Radio Address
entitled "Children in a Democracy," FDR
said, "I have read a book recently; it is
called *The Grapes of Wrath*. There are
500,000 Americans that live in the
covers of that book…Migratory families,
children who have no homes, families
who can put down no roots, cannot live
in a community…

I am trying to find a place for them to go."

Makeshift merchants sell
apples on New York's 42nd
Street. Said one seller,
"People mostly hurry by, as if
they don't want to look at y

Too poor to ride, an Arkansas
family walks through Texas
looking for work in the
Rio Grande cotton fields,
a trek of about 900 miles.

The Second Term
1937–1941

The second room in the Memorial presents visitors with powerful and jarring images, confronting them with the realities of a country sunk in unemployment, despair, and poverty with no social or financial safety nets to depend upon for help. Neither government nor the private sector had mechanisms to respond to the overwhelming need. There was no social security, unemployment insurance, medical care, workers' compensation, or help for the aged.

The dual nature of the second-term room depicts both the enormous problems posed by the Great Depression and the New Deal programs for resolving these problems. As visitors enter this space, sculptures and quotations communicate the deep frustrations and despair affecting both rural and urban America. On the far side of the dividing wall, however, a thirty-foot-long bronze mural depicting fifty-four of the social programs reveals the New Deal response. These programs were developed to give employment, to reverse the downward momentum of the Depression, and to enable people to engage in work projects which would give them a sense of pride and accomplishment.

The farm couple

The fountain is patterned after one of the Tennesse valley authority dams & symbolizes the first great regional electrification projects of the new Deal...

This grill window gives a view across to the Potomac

grill

Man listening to a fireside chat on his Philco radio

3 Segal sculptures

an breadline

Halprin

As visitors emerge from the garden passageway and enter the second-term room, they will see an alcove set into the granite wall. This recessed niche implies an indoor setting. It is human-scale and private and appears to give passers-by a glimpse into someone's home. In this room sits a sculpture of an average-looking man entranced by the voice coming from his Philco radio. He is listening with intense concentration and hope to the words of his president.

It was through these "Fireside Chats" that FDR spoke with the American people. Hearing his voice over the radio in their living rooms, they felt as if he was visiting with them personally.

FDR delivers a "Fireside Chat" on December 29, 1940.

"I NEVER FORGET THAT I LIVE IN A HOUSE OWNED BY ALL THE AMERICAN PEOPLE AND THAT I HAVE BEEN GIVEN THEIR TRUST."

Steven Schoenherr described the importance of FDR's ability to communicate in his lecture *FDR and the Media*, which he delivered to the Smithsonian Institution in 1977:

"'FIRESIDE CHATS' were given their name by the Press. Radio speeches given by FDR which were to be intimate talks with the American people to explain issues in their government were given this name. They were informal evening broadcasts to the whole American public. There were never formal announcements. FDR saw them as a way to educate the public and he loved to be the teacher. FDR often used analogy in Fireside Chats to make complex points or controversial points appear simple. FDR used the address 'My friends' to open the Fireside Chats and immediately bound the friendship of his radio audiences. No president had ever addressed the public with this phrase."

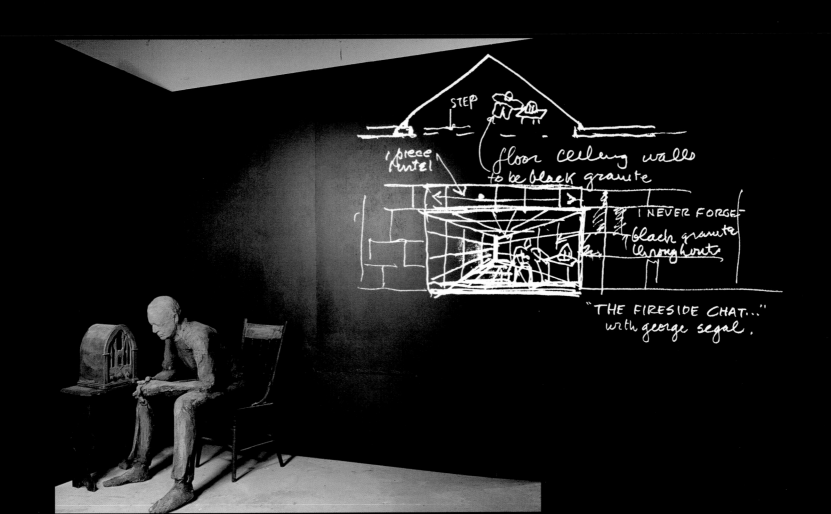

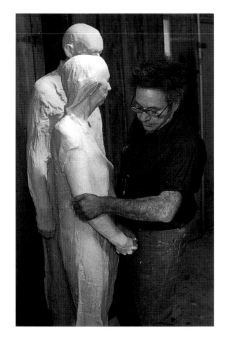

George Segal adjusts an early plaster maquette of *Appalachian Couple*. In this early stage the woman is standing; in the final design she is seated.

Turning away from this historic scene, visitors encounter two more sculptural vignettes by GEORGE SEGAL which exemplify the overwhelming issue of poverty. One scene captures a farm couple caught in what appears to be an unending cycle of despair. They appear in front of their barn, their only obvious possession a wooden chair.

GEORGE SEGAL was born in the Bronx, New York City, in 1924. His parents had immigrated from eastern Europe. George exhibited an interest in art early and won honors for his work while still in high school. George was raised in New Jersey, where his family settled, and he helped his parents with their chicken-raising business throughout his teens. Later, he took over the farm and still lives there with his wife Helen. Today, the old chicken coops house his art studio.

Everyday life and everyday happenings form the basis of George Segal's sculptures. His pieces are cast directly from live models, mostly friends and relatives. George's method of sculpting is unique. It depends heavily on real-life events and people set within environments which he constructs from real elements and furnishings. Segal's work is therefore figurative but it does not romanticize or idealize the people whom he casts.

As the critic Phyllis Tuckman explains in the book, *George Segal: Recent Painted Sculpture*, "Segal's figures radiate an aura of the familiar. They look like the kind of people with whom you come in daily contact.... These slices of life's scenarios belie or mask other aspects of this haunting art." Segal's environments express more than what is visible on the surface. They dig deeply and say much about the universal elements of life through their focus on simple tasks.

It was for these reasons that George Segal was chosen to work within the themes of the Memorial. George has strong feelings and deep empathy for the Roosevelt era. He quickly selected three everyday images that were descriptive of the essence of the Depression years in our country, which had such a deep influence on the character and quality of our culture. Within these depictions the message is one of inherent individual dignity in the face of overwhelming odds.

George Segal developed his very personal casting technique in the early 1960s. He starts by dipping cloth bandages in wet plaster and then applying them directly to a body or to an object. He spends time working with his models before casting, describing the gestures he is trying to achieve and choreographing the positioning of their bodies in space within the constructed environment. Artist and model work together to finalize the pose before wrapping begins. Once the format

has been fixed, the bandages are fitted around the various parts of the body. Hardening takes only minutes and then the bandages are removed by splitting them into sections. Later, they are reassembled to form the final figures or, as was the case for figures in the Memorial, they become molds for the final bronze sculptures.

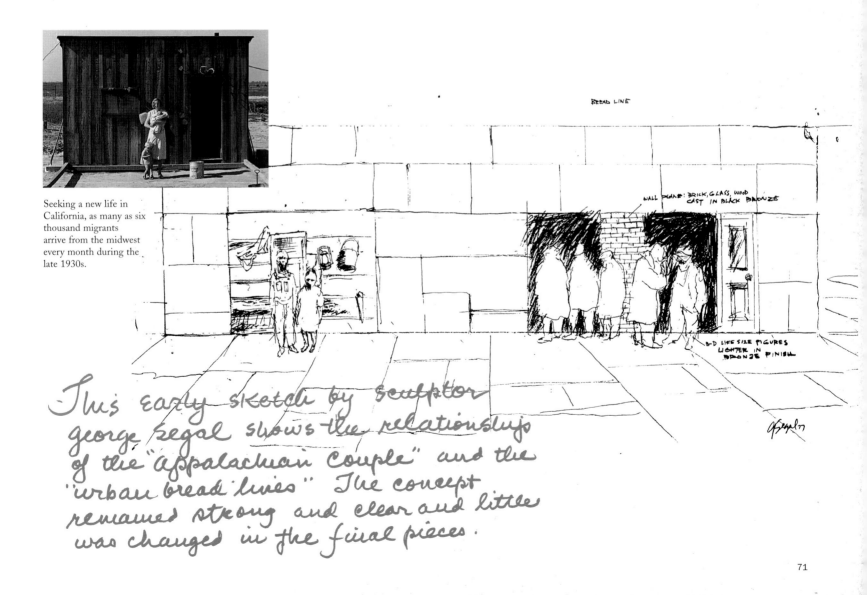

Seeking a new life in California, as many as six thousand migrants arrive from the midwest every month during the late 1930s.

This early sketch by sculptor George Segal shows the relationship of the "appalachian couple" and the "urban bread lines" The concept remained strong and clear and little was changed in the final pieces.

In researching the specific elements of "The Breadline" George Segal found coats and hats from the Era, which he clothed his models in, as he wrapped this sculpture.

The homeless and the unemployed
wait in a food line in Chicago.
November 1930.

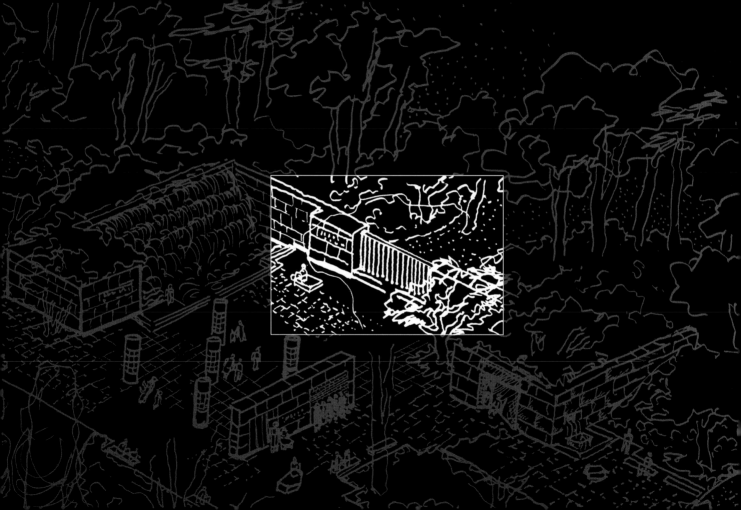

Up to this point, the Memorial has been
introverted and enclosed but a window
in this outdoor room offers some
relief with its view toward the west,
toward the Potomac River. The window
allows the sun to brighten the room
with additional light and it allows
those who pass in the secular world
beyond a glimpse into the Memorial and
into these historic times.

The Tennessee Valley Authority inspired the fountain in this room.

A waterfall, full of harnessed energy,

represents the program which resulted in the electrification
of a whole agricultural region, the development of flood control,
demonstration farms, and extension services for farmers.

Early in his presidency, FDR had asked Congress for legislation
for an agency which would be charged with the duty of planning for the
proper use, conservation, and development of the natural resources of the
Tennessee River drainage basin and its adjoining territory.
In this speech, FDR said,

"IT IS TIME TO EXTEND PLANNING TO A WIDER FIELD,

IN THIS INSTANCE COMPREHENDING IN ONE GREAT PROJECT

MANY STATES DIRECTLY CONCERNED WITH

THE BASIN OF ONE OF OUR GREATEST RIVERS."

Suggestion for Legislation to Create the TVA
April 10, 1933

I PROPOSE TO CREAT
CONSERVATION CORPS
WORK... MORE IMPOR
THE MATERIAL GAIN
AND SPIRITUAL VALUE

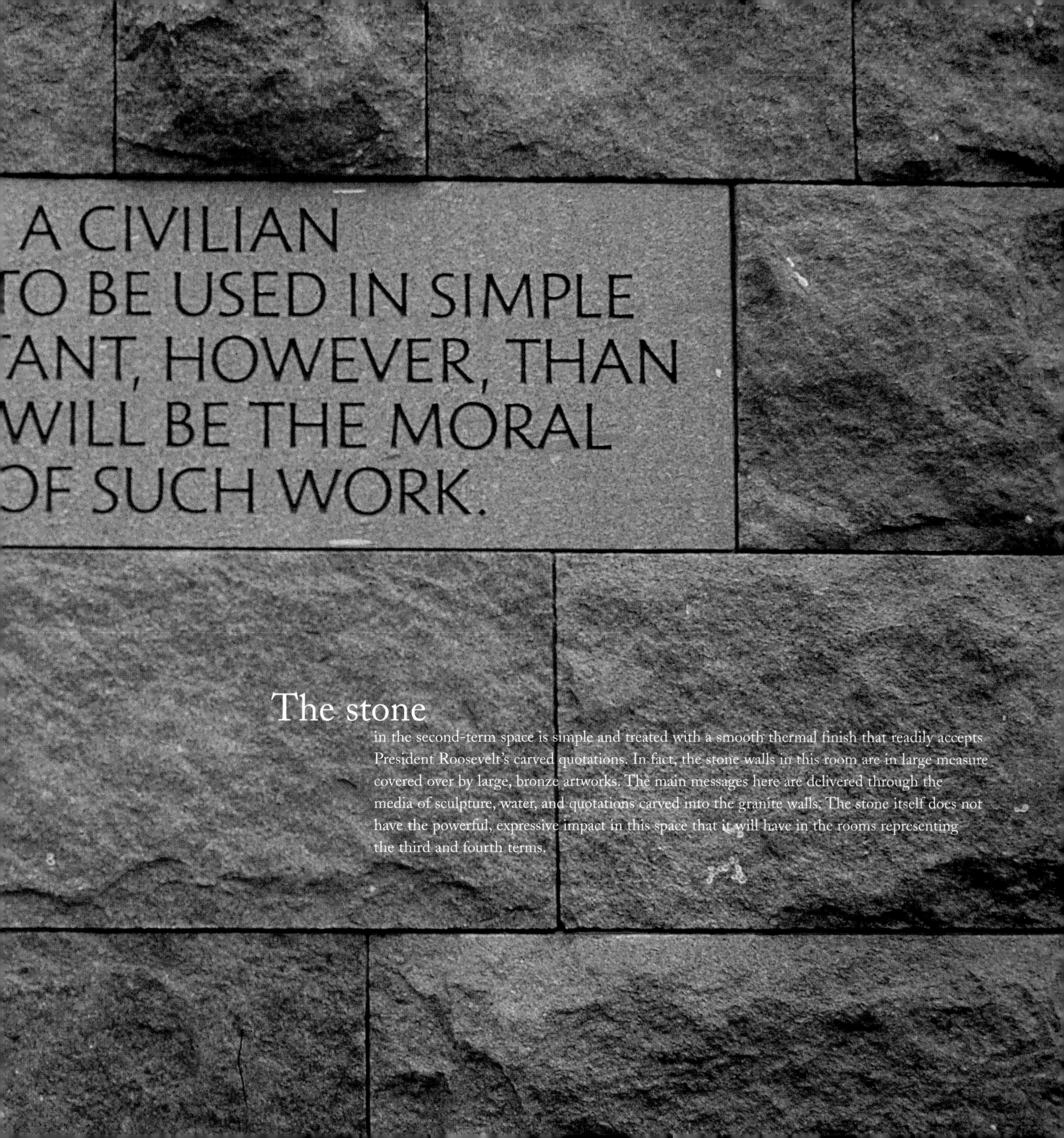

A CIVILIAN
TO BE USED IN SIMPLE
TANT, HOWEVER, THAN
WILL BE THE MORAL
OF SUCH WORK.

The stone

in the second-term space is simple and treated with a smooth thermal finish that readily accepts President Roosevelt's carved quotations. In fact, the stone walls in this room are in large measure covered over by large, bronze artworks. The main messages here are delivered through the media of sculpture, water, and quotations carved into the granite walls. The stone itself does not have the powerful, expressive impact in this space that it will have in the rooms representing the third and fourth terms.

A multitude of New Deal efforts are further memorialized in this chamber in the form of a
THIRTY-FOOT-LONG BRONZE MURAL BY ROBERT GRAHAM.

"I PROPOSE TO CREATE

Shown on these two pages are details from Robert Graham's *Social Programs* bas-relief.

ROBERT GRAHAM began his study for the *Social Programs* mural by doing intensive research on the New Deal. He chose fifty-four programs to depict and then looked for images to graphically symbolize the essence of each. Thus, for example, the Civilian Conservation Corps (CCC) is symbolized by two workers planting a ponderosa pine seedling, and the Farm Security Administration (FSA), by a farmer driving a tractor.

The mural consists of realistic images as well as writing, braille, and a background of the hands and faces of workers. The mural depicts the efforts of many of the innovative programs— the CCC, the WPA, the TVA, the FSA, labor relations, social security—which elevated the country from the quagmire into which it had sunk. These social programs, sometimes called the alphabet programs (because of the acronyms which referred to them), were the New Deal solutions which were developed to enable people to pull themselves up from the depths of despair.

"A CIVILIAN CONSERVATION CORPS
TO BE USED IN SIMPLE WORK...
MORE IMPORTANT, HOWEVER, THAN THE MATERIAL
GAINS WILL BE THE MORAL AND SPIRITUAL VALUE
OF SUCH WORK."

One of the jobs performed
by members of the Civilian
Conservation Corps was
clearing away downed trees
for reforestation projects.

Many of the programs FDR initiated were also linked to President Roosevelt's
ongoing interests in conservation, reforestation, and rural electrification.
The link between these interests and the unemployment crisis led to his
suggestion for a Civilian Conservation Corps.

The next step for sculptor Graham was to establish an overall format for the mural that would organize all of the images. Graham used a grid of photographs as a way to study this issue. The result is a matrix based on a twelve-by-twelve-inch grid of squares overlaid on five 6-by-6-foot panels. One panel contains thirty-six 12-inch squares, two panels contain nine 24-inch squares, and two panels contain four 36-inch squares. Within this geometry, the mural allows for a series of variations within an overall order.

Born in Mexico, Graham came to the United States in 1950 when he was twelve years old. He studied at the San Francisco Art Institute, where the great muralist Diego Rivera had taught.

Since the 1970s, Graham's sculptures have shifted from beautiful, small, gallery-sized environments to large monument-scale civic works such as the gateway figures at the 1984 Los Angeles Olympics and the Duke Ellington Memorial in New York's Central Park.

Bob works primarily in bronze and has his own foundry where he often casts his pieces with his production team. This workshop approach to the making of art is very reminiscent of Renaissance artists and has allowed him to experiment and explore new materials and casting techniques. Masterful draftsmanship of the human form, innovative casting techniques, and an appreciation of architecture as an art of spaces as well as of forms have allowed Bob Graham to envision his sculptures as part of an expanded public life.

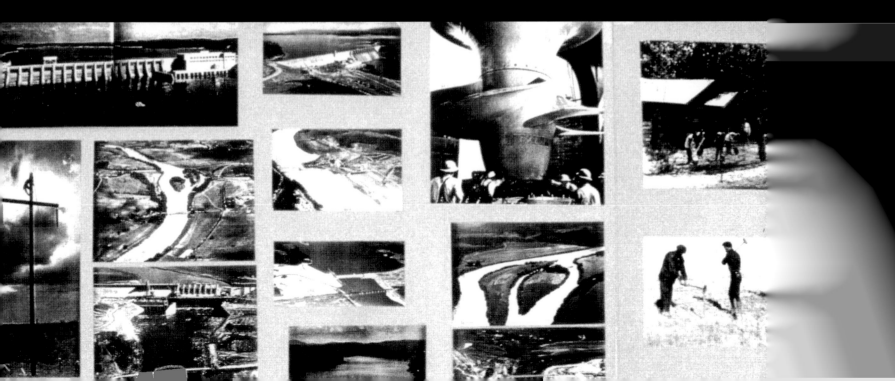

Bob Graham and Halprin
study the placement of
the bronze cylinders on a
small-scale mock-up.

Graham's murals sympathetically evoke
the Works Progress Administration
murals of the New Deal. The WPA
funded highly creative, unemployed
artists to work on government
buildings. The murals, which often
depict workers engaged in their labor,
enriched the quality of post offices,
libraries, and other civic buildings.

In addition to the mural itself, Graham devised an innovative method of revealing the casting process and further exploring the images. Five bronze cylinders stand free from the wall and contain the negative images of the five panels on the large wall.

A viewer can imagine these cylinder seals rolled onto clay to make the positive images on the murals affixed to the wall. And, as a metaphor, the viewer can imagine the positive, practical results produced by these alphabet agencies.

ROLL OUT

The seals cylinder

The Bronze wall social programs mural

Five columns positioned in front of the bronze mural depict the social program images in their negative form. These columns are similar to sculptural cylinder seals ... the type used for centuries by sculptors to roll across clay in the making of bas reliefs.

The bronze cylinders shown in this early study model are rendered in maquette form.

As visitors prepare to leave the second-term room, they enter a passageway which leads them toward room three. This passageway provides the same kind of quiet, contemplative space as did the first passageway. It slopes upward and there is a heavy, somber planting of pine trees on the horizon. There is, however, a suggestion of a new threat, an external one.

In this passageway,
President Roosevelt speaks to the threat.

"WE MUST SCRUPULOUSLY GUARD THE CIVIL RIGHTS
AND CIVIL LIBERTIES OF ALL CITIZENS,
WHATEVER THEIR BACKGROUND.
WE MUST REMEMBER THAT ANY OPPRESSION,
ANY INJUSTICE, ANY HATRED, IS A WEDGE DESIGNED
TO ATTACK OUR CIVILIZATION."

**Letter to the American Committee
for Protection of Foreign-born**
January 9, 1940

FDR accepts his
third-term nomination.

As the 1930s wore on, the desperate need for America's help in Europe became ever more obvious to the president, as well as others. Winston Churchill made this need abundantly clear during his many visits to the White House. The German invasions of Norway and the low countries of Europe confirmed the urgency of the situation. This was the beginning of a new period in our history, a period of increasing threat and conflict from abroad.

The United States, however, was not yet ready to enter the war. The struggle to pull ourselves out of the Depression had led to a strong sense of isolationism, and many people felt that this country should worry about itself and let the rest of the world do the same. President Roosevelt had to provide help cautiously. He developed several ways of helping without stepping over the line and committing the country to entering the war.

One of FDR's strategies was the Lend-Lease Act. Britain desperately needed destroyers to combat the submarine war against shipping. In September 1940 the president informed Congress that "this Government has acquired the right to lease naval and air bases in Newfoundland, and in the islands of Bermuda, the Bahamas, Jamaica, St. Lucia, Trinidad, and Antigua, and in British Guiana…

"The right to bases in Newfoundland and Bermuda are gifts—generously given and gladly received. The other bases mentioned have been acquired in exchange for fifty of our over-age destroyers."

The war, however, continued to worsen as more countries were invaded. FDR finally took a determined step. This time the help we offered was unconstrained. In a "Fireside Chat" on national security, delivered on December 29, 1940, President Roosevelt said,

"I want to make it clear that it is the purpose of the nation to build now with all possible speed every machine, every arsenal, every factory that we need to manufacture our defense material. We have the men—the skill—the wealth— and above all the will."

There is a solemn quality, a foreboding in the passageway because of the growing dangers of war. As visitors move through, they will encounter a narrow cascade of water emerging from a fissure in the granite wall. The fissure hints at the looming shadow of the future—the shadow of a split, a break, a powerful eruption. Entering the third-term room, visitors encounter FDR's quote about the need to guard ourselves against attack and enslavement:

"WE MUST BE THE GREAT ARSENAL OF DEMOCRACY."

The German army
advances on Warsaw, Poland,
September 1, 1939.

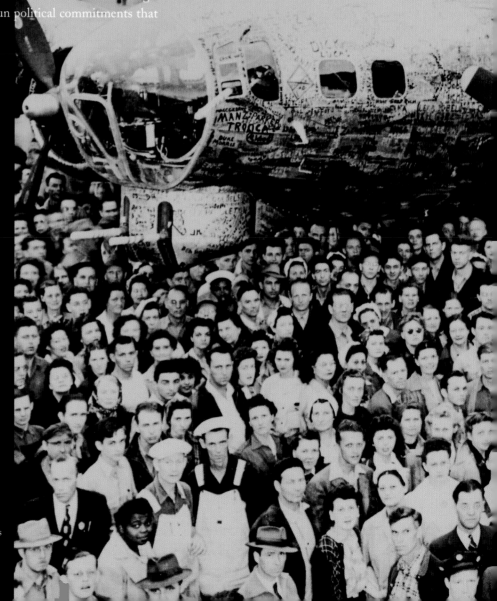

IN 1941, FDR ENTERED HIS THIRD TERM OF OFFICE. Through the Lend-Lease Act, the United States had continued to increase its efforts to supply the Allied countries with destroyers, planes, and the tools and weapons they needed to defend themselves against the Axis powers. The war, however, was worsening, and FDR knew that these efforts were not nearly enough.

In August 1941, FDR sailed into the north Atlantic to meet Prime Minister Winston Churchill aboard the battleship *Prince of Wales*. During the four days of this Atlantic Charter Conference, they talked about the war in Europe. By mid-1941 the British had lost 1,500 ships—all sunk by German submarines. There was already an undeclared war between the United States and Germany, and our destroyers were escorting British convoys crossing the Atlantic. Churchill emphasized that what was at stake was the survival of civilization as we knew it.

FDR was growing increasingly concerned about the international situation and the war in Europe. Yet within the country and the houses of Congress there was still a strong mood of isolationism. FDR had to choose his words carefully and seek out opportunities to promote his approach to international policy. In 1933 he had dedicated our nation to the Good Neighbor Policy and had determined that the United States would shun political commitments that would draw it into foreign wars.

FDR and Churchill aboard the HMS *Prince of Wales* during the Atlantic Charter Conference in Placentia Bay, Newfoundland. August 10, 1941.

Boeing Aircraft celebrates the 5,000th B-17 as it leaves the production line in Seattle, Washington. 1944.

On August 14, 1936, in Chautauqua, New York, FDR expressed his abhorrence of all war when he gave a speech dedicated to peace:

"I HAVE SEEN WAR.

I HAVE SEEN WAR ON LAND AND SEA.

I HAVE SEEN BLOOD RUNNING FROM THE WOUNDED...

I HAVE SEEN THE DEAD IN THE MUD.

I HAVE SEEN CITIES DESTROYED...

I HAVE SEEN CHILDREN STARVING.

I HAVE SEEN THE AGONY OF MOTHERS AND WIVES.

I HATE WAR."

These words, which captured the horrors of a commitment to war, are emblazoned across the granite wall in the third-term room.

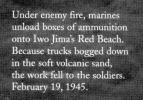

Under enemy fire, marines unload boxes of ammunition onto Iwo Jima's Red Beach. Because trucks bogged down in the soft volcanic sand, the work fell to the soldiers. February 19, 1945.

The Third Term
1941–1945

Visitors are confronted by a great
destructive presence as they move out of
the passageway and into the third-term
room. Giant granite blocks are strewn
across the paved pathway. Looking about,
they will realize that the destruction
emanates from the walls and the fountain.
The rubble is meant to represent the impact
that a bomb would have on the walls and
fountain if it exploded in the room. Great
fragments of the wall lie askew on the
pavement. Pipes are broken and water
spurts from amidst fragments. The feeling is
reminiscent of the war years in Europe.
It recalls scenes of horrible bombing and
destruction in London, Dresden, Warsaw,
and other cities. The atmosphere of armed
conflict and the effects of war in this room
are overpowering and unsettling.

The top stones of the fountain are broken as if struck by a bomb

I HATE WAR

THE WAR WALL

Halprin

Empty streets and crumbling
buildings are all that are
left after enemy bombing of
an English village. 1940.

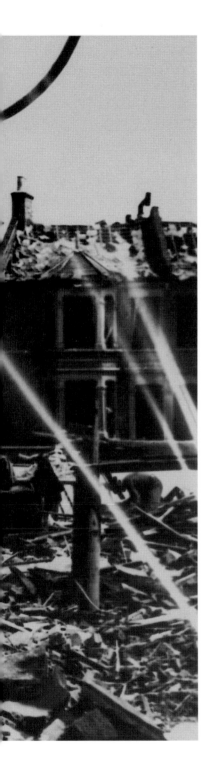

The United States was not officially at war until Japan launched a surprise offensive and attacked the Hawaiian Islands, Hong Kong, Guam, the Philippine Islands, Wake Island, and Midway Island. Japan's carrier-based bombers destroyed American battleships, cruisers, destroyers, and planes, and killed over 2,400 men at Pearl Harbor, Hawaii, in the early morning attack.

The effect was devastating. On December 8, 1941, President Roosevelt delivered a six-minute address to Congress in which he said: "Yesterday, December 7, 1941—a date which will live in infamy—the United States was suddenly and deliberately attacked by naval and air forces of the Empire of Japan....As commander in chief of the army and navy, I have directed that measures be taken for our defense."

The next day, December 9, 1941, President Roosevelt spoke to the nation by way of a "Fireside Chat" and explained our position.

"We are now in this war. We are all in it—all the way. Every single man, woman, and child is a partner in the most tremendous undertaking of our American history."

Several days later, Germany joined Japan and declared war on the United States.

The USS *West Virginia* and USS *Tennessee* lie in ruins after the Japanese attack at Pearl Harbor on December 7, 1941.

I HAVE SEEN WAR

I HAVE SEEN WAR ON LAND AND SEA
BLOOD RUNNING FROM THE WOUND
SEEN THE DEAD IN THE MUD. I HAVE
DESTROYED... I HAVE SEEN CHILDRE
I HAVE SEEN THE AGONY OF MOT

I HATE WAR

The War Wall is in position.
The stones in the foreground
carry the refrain from
FDR's quote "I hate war."

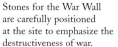

Stones for the War Wall
are carefully positioned
at the site to emphasize the
destructiveness of war.

In designing the Memorial, the sculptors and I worried over the question of how to depict the war—how to express its devastating impact on the whole world. That was the most difficult challenge of the entire memorial narrative for us.

WE WANTED TO EXPRESS THE DICHOTOMY—

the absolute necessity of entering the fight
as well as the repellent horror of a war that would take the
lives of tens of millions of men, women, and children
throughout the world.

The outcome of all our attempts to express this war—the result of our sketches and discussions and frustrations—is this room, which reveals the brutal forces of bombs. President Roosevelt's words are carved into the wall behind the rubble and drift down onto the granite blocks as if at random. In this way, the words and the wall remind us all of the holocaust. Worldwide destruction is here made manifest.

The use of a clay model of the fountain and War Wall in room three enables Halprin to visualize the relationship of the water effects and the placement of stones before the final installation.

The stones in this room carry much of the message. These blocks are larger and rougher and more primitive than the walls in the earlier rooms. They are like giant shards broken from the great wall by brute force and strewn at chaotic angles. That implied force stands for all the forces of evil visited on the world at the time of World War II.

The water interacts with the stones and echoes the destructive message. The flow is not calming; it is not meant to soothe as water usually does. The water here strikes broken edges and ricochets off in wild directions as if chaotically caused by the war. The backdrop for this agitated room is a dark and somber planting of pine trees on the skyline, behind the fountain.

Several great granite blocks lean
against the broken wall in
the third-term room fountain.
The skyline is jagged with
broken blocks, symbolizing
war damage.

These details of the fountain
show various water effects that
suggest broken piping. Water jets
ricochet in chaotic directions.

WE HAVE FAITH THAT FUTURE GENERATIONS WILL KNOW THAT HERE, IN THE MIDDLE OF THE TWENTIETH CENTURY, THERE CAME A TIME WHEN MEN OF GOOD WILL FOUND A WAY TO UNITE, AND PRODUCE, AND FIGHT TO DESTROY THE FORCES OF IGNORANCE, AND INTOLERANCE, AND SLAVERY, AND WAR.

To the left of the fountain, the pines provide a dark green foliage frame for a bronze portrait of the president. It portrays him at Hyde Park, New York, toward the end of the war. The niche emphasizes his strength and confidence; it frames the portrait and is especially enhanced by a massive anchor stone.

This stone is twenty-nine feet long and six feet high. The stone symbolizes the great power of the presidency; it evokes feelings of strength and fortitude.

This stone represents the fundamental greatness of a man who has carried the tremendous challenges and responsibilities of the war on his shoulders.

Neil Estern captures the details of FDR's chair. The flowered decorations—which were specially designed for the Roosevelt family—and the casters on the chair legs are carefully re-created in the final maquette.

Fala, FDR's Scottish terrier, his treasured and constant companion, is seated at his feet in the portrait. Even during the most difficult of times, FDR kept his good humor, and the image of Fala is a reminder of this aspect of his personality.

Fala is joined by FDR in the study. Washington, December 20, 1941.

This powerful portrayal of President Roosevelt was created by sculptor NEIL ESTERN, a resident of Brooklyn, New York.

This detail of FDR's hands comes from an early clay model by Neil Estern.

His work here captures all of the details of FDR that animated his personality—the energy, the exuberance, the wrinkles, the tilts of the head, the gestures, and the body language.

The sculptor's intent is that the viewer not only recognize the character of the man, but also the aura of his personality.

Estern went to great lengths to research this portrait of FDR. At Hyde Park, once the president's home and now a museum, Estern was able to study, photograph, and measure individual elements that appear in the sculpture. The chair is a replica in bronze of the one that FDR used to move around in at Hyde Park.

The closures on FDR's cape and the way the material folds and drapes are also depicted with great care. FDR's left leg is cast in such a way as to reveal its weakness and immobility. Nevertheless, the president is steadfast in his attitude. It is clear that he is strong and purposeful in the face of this war. His eyes gaze ahead to the future. On the wall, adjacent to his image, is another quotation from one of FDR's determined speeches.

GIs leave a landing craft
under heavy enemy fire.
Omaha Beach, Normandy,
June 6, 1944.

On March 15, 1941, early in his third term, FDR had accepted an invitation to address the annual dinner of the White House Correspondents' Association. This was the first time in his eight years as president that he had made a speech to this influential group. The members were accustomed to a question-and-answer press conference, not a speech.

FDR captured the attention of his audience by beginning: "Before the present war broke out on September 1, 1939, I was more worried about the future than many people— indeed, than most people. The record shows that I was not worried enough."

The president went on to emphasize the seriousness of the situation: "Nazi forces are not seeking mere modifications in colonial maps or in minor European boundaries. They openly seek the destruction of all elective systems of government on every continent—including our own;

THEY (WHO) SEEK TO ESTABLISH SYSTEMS OF GOVERNMENT BASED ON THE REGIMENTATION OF ALL HUMAN BEINGS BY A HANDFUL OF INDIVIDUAL RULERS... CALL THIS A NEW ORDER. IT IS NOT NEW AND IT IS NOT ORDER."

FRANKLIN DELANO ROOSEVELT'S THIRD TERM WAS WHOLLY DEVOTED TO WINNING THIS WORLD WAR AND THEN WORKING TOWARD A LASTING PEACE.

In 1943, when he revisited the White House Correspondents' Association, the president updated the group on the situation of the war. Uppermost in his mind was "…our determination to fight this war to the finish—to the day when united nations' forces march in triumph through the streets of Berlin, and Rome, and Tokyo."

On his return from the Cairo-Teheran Conference, FDR stops over and meets with General Dwight D. Eisenhower (right) at an air strip in Sicily. December 8, 1943.

The president was confident and firm as he ended his speech with these words:

"WE HAVE FAITH THAT FUTURE GENERATIONS
WILL KNOW THAT HERE, IN THE MIDDLE
OF THE TWENTIETH CENTURY,
THERE CAME A TIME WHEN MEN OF GOOD WILL
FOUND A WAY TO UNITE, AND PRODUCE,
AND FIGHT TO DESTROY
THE FORCES OF IGNORANCE,
AND INTOLERANCE, AND SLAVERY, AND WAR."

AS VISITORS MOVE FROM THE THIRD OUTDOOR ROOM TO THE FOURTH,
they travel from the end of FDR's third term in office to his reelection for an unprecedented fourth
term. The war was winding down. The last of the wartime conferences held by the leaders of the
Alliance, the Yalta Conference, was scheduled to be held in the Crimea in early February 1945.

The campaign for FDR's fourth term was difficult, and FDR's health became a major issue.
Thomas Dewey, the opposition candidate, ran on a platform based in large measure on the age and
ill health of the president and his cabinet.

FDR, however, was a great campaigner. The success of the battles in the Philippines and General
MacArthur's landing there were being acclaimed. The final result at the polls was a victory and
a fourth term for FDR. In accordance with his usual ritual, the president listened to the results on
the radio at his home in Hyde Park, New York. He visited with neighbors on the porch,
his flowing cape draped over his shoulders to ward off the chill.

The Fourth Term
1945

There is no garden passageway between the third- and fourth-term rooms of the Memorial. The war, the peace, and the effects of FDR's untimely death were all unfolding in a whirlwind. Newsreels, radio broadcasts, and banner headlines delivered history-making news on a daily basis. The two theaters of war competed for attention. Life was being lived at a very fast pace.

Therefore, as visitors move from the third- to the fourth-term room, they find themselves on a viewing platform rather than in a tranquil passageway. The overlook provides a way of looking forward at what lies ahead as well as back to the recent past. The fourth room is dedicated to peace and an optimistic view of the future. It is consecrated to the achievement of FDR's enlightened ideals.

THE 4 FREEDOMS

view to Jefferson

FREEDOM FROM FEAR
FREEDOM FROM WANT
FREEDOM OF WORSHIP
FREEDOM OF SPEECH

The Eleanor niche

The overlook

Halprin

Shortly after taking his oath of office, FDR set sail for the Soviet Crimea. There, on February 4, 1945, the eight-day Yalta Conference opened. At Yalta, the attention of the three great leaders of the Allies (Churchill, Roosevelt, and Stalin) began to shift from the winning of the war itself to the winning of the peace.

Churchill and Stalin jockeyed for position and negotiated about the future in terms of political power and their influence on the small countries. They questioned who would dominate in the Balkans, in Greece, Turkey, and Poland.

Churchill was primarily interested in the preservation of the British Empire and worried about the spread of world communism.

Stalin was intent on the expansion of communism in Europe.

FDR, however, kept his sights on how to achieve a just and lasting peace.

At his March 1, 1945, address to Congress on the outcome of Yalta, FDR was enthusiastic about the future. He promised that a conference of all the united nations of the world would meet in San Francisco on April 25, 1945.

FDR's health, however, had begun to worsen.

At Yalta he had appeared weakened and haggard, even though his spirits were high. When he delivered his report on the Conference to the joint houses of Congress, he acknowledged his disability for the first time in public and excused himself for not standing during his address.

"I hope you will pardon me for the unusual posture of sitting down during the presentation of what I want to say, but I know that you will realize that it makes it a lot easier for me not to have to carry about ten pounds of steel around on the bottom of my legs; and also because of the fact that I have just completed a 14,000-mile trip."

Churchill, Roosevelt,
and Stalin meet at the
Yalta Conference in early
February 1945.

To make reference to his disability was difficult for FDR, since he had gone to such great lengths to hide it. For years there had been a gentlemen's agreement among photographers and the press: no mention was made of FDR's physical condition and no photographs were published of his wheelchair or of him being carried out of his car. Newsreels always showed him apparently walking on his own while in reality he was supported by his sons or associates.

After the long and difficult trip to Yalta and his address to Congress, FDR went to Warm Springs, Georgia to rest, recuperate, and work on the Jefferson Day speech that he was to deliver on April 13. In that speech he wanted to focus on his vision for the future and the great and lasting peace he sought to achieve. His major premise was stated clearly in the following words:

"MORE THAN AN END TO WAR, WE WANT AN END TO THE BEGINNINGS OF ALL WAR."

Those words are carved in twelve-inch letters on the granite wall between the third and fourth rooms of the Memorial. They are carefully placed in an area where there is a major confluence— an intersection of the movement within the Memorial. This is a place for all visitors to stop and consider the power of this basic idea, which is also the basis of the United Nations.

IT IS A STATEMENT OF CONVICTION, it is absolutely necessary to end all wars.

FDR was not able to deliver those words. On April 12, 1945, he died at Warm Springs.

On a profound level, FDR's death recalls the death of the biblical prophet Moses, who brought the Israelites to the border of the land of milk and honey but was not himself allowed to enter. FDR had achieved his goal of freeing the world from the menace of dictatorships. The Allies had essentially won the war, but FDR did not live to enjoy the peace that was declared in Europe on May 8, 1945, and in Japan on August 15, 1945.

As visitors move beyond the fourth room overlook, they are drawn to a walkway gently sloping down to the right. The ramp leads toward an intimate sunken alcove—a space dedicated to FDR's death.

An early working model of the funeral alcove shows an aerial view of the pool reflecting the bronze mural of the cortege.

This funeral alcove has been set below the level of the third-term room.

The drop in elevation emphasizes its separation from the rest of the Memorial.

It is a realm of empathy and finality.

A THIRTY-FOOT-LONG BRONZE BAS-RELIEF, *Funeral Cortege,*
graces the end wall of this confined and sorrowful space.

The bronze depicts FDR's funeral procession as it moved ceremoniously up Pennsylvania Avenue to the Capitol. The catafalque is drawn by four horses, and in the background weeping mourners trudge in the wake of their beloved president. These people were experiencing the loss of a beloved member of their family, as well as of the leader who had brought them through more than a decade of pain and uncertainty.

The bas-relief captures, in a somber and powerful way, the emotions of the day. The great bronze piece is mirrored in a reflecting pool, and just as the bronze depiction memorializes FDR's death, the mirrored image in the pool symbolizes the profound reflective effect the president's death had on the American people.

The sculptor of *Funeral Cortege,* LEONARD BASKIN, is an artist in many expressive media. A master

printmaker, draftsman, and book designer, he is perhaps most highly acclaimed for his sculpture. Baskin's art is concerned with the viewer's release of sympathetic feelings and emotions triggered by the forms, situations, expressions, and subjects he creates. He constantly strives to immerse himself in the impact of the situations he sculpts. In Funeral Cortege, the sculptor depicts not only the cortege itself, but the influence FDR's death had on the nation.

At his art foundry in Brooklyn, New York, Leonard Baskin studies the interim plaster mold of *Funeral Cortege* before it is finally cast in bronze.

Throngs of tearful mourners lined Pennsylvania Avenue to honor President Roosevelt as they watched the catafalque slowly pass by on April 14, 1945.

As visitors leave this somber alcove and move farther down along the ramp, they encounter another reminder of FDR's last quest. Carefully framed in rough-hewn stone are FDR's prophetic words:

"UNLESS THE PEACE THAT FOLLOWS RECOGNIZES THAT THE WHOLE WORLD IS ONE NEIGHBORHOOD AND DOES JUSTICE TO THE WHOLE HUMAN RACE, THE GERMS OF ANOTHER WORLD WAR WILL REMAIN AS A CONSTANT THREAT TO MANKIND."

FDR uttered these words at an address to the White House Correspondents' Association on February 12, 1943.

Turning from the wall and continuing down from the funeral alcove, visitors once again have a powerful view of the Washington Monument. This view, which reappears throughout the Memorial, reconnects the Memorial to the historic bedrock on which the country was founded.

Visitors catch a glimpse of the Washington Monument across the Tidal Basin as they leave the funeral alcove.

At the bottom of the ramp there is a niche in the wall containing a sculpture of ELEANOR ROOSEVELT by Neil Estern. Estern, who sculpted the seated image of FDR in the third room, portrays Mrs. Roosevelt here as our first delegate to the newly established United Nations.

A sculpture of Eleanor Roosevelt stands as if emerging from the United Nations headquarters. On the wall above her head is the emblem of the United Nations.

To the left of the niche there is a quotation from FDR's March 1, 1945, address to Congress on the Yalta Conference.

"THE STRUCTURE OF WORLD PEACE
CANNOT BE THE WORK OF ONE MAN,
OR ONE PARTY, OR ONE NATION...
IT MUST BE A PEACE WHICH RESTS
ON THE COOPERATIVE EFFORT OF
THE WHOLE WORLD."

Eleanor Roosevelt was the ideal person to carry FDR's vision into the future after the years of war. Mrs. Roosevelt was more than FDR's wife and First Lady of the nation.

During the long years of his presidency, she had been FDR's partner, his social conscience, his eyes and ears, and his messenger to the rest of the world.

Eleanor had perceived the presidency as a platform from which to advance major improvements in the areas of social programs, community action, working conditions, and child labor laws. As the imperative of the war took the center stage of FDR's presidency, Eleanor struggled hard to prevent the country from backsliding on the important and far-reaching social advances that had been achieved.

Mrs. Roosevelt comforts a wounded soldier during a 1943 visit to the South Pacific. In a letter to a friend before the trip, she wrote, "Where I do see our soldiers, I'll try to make them feel that Franklin really wants to know about them."

The fourth room speaks to the future that FDR envisioned. Roosevelt had kept his eye on the need for world wide peace. He knew that such a peace would depend on the participation of all nations and had worried over how to achieve it. In a brilliant series of moves, FDR pushed the United Nations in that direction.

FDR emphasized the depth of his determination in his final days. At his congressional address on Yalta, he said, *"This time we are not making the mistake of waiting until the end of the war to set up the machinery of peace. This time, as we fight together to win the war finally, we work together to keep it from happening again."*

The view of the Jefferson Memorial from the fourth room is seen here through the cherry trees along the Tidal Basin.

In the fourth room, visitors for the first time become aware of the Jefferson Memorial in the distance. The speech that FDR was working on at Warm Springs, Georgia, immediately before his death was to have been dedicated to peace and in honor of President Thomas Jefferson, a man FDR greatly admired.

FDR devoted much of his Jefferson Day speech to the need to "cultivate the science of human relations—the ability of all peoples, of all kinds, to live together and work together, in the same world, at peace." The last words which FDR wrote by hand into the typed draft of this speech were,

"THE ONLY LIMIT TO OUR REALIZATION OF TOMORROW WILL BE OUR DOUBTS OF TODAY.

LET US MOVE FORWARD

The last written words of the president echo the theme he enunciated twelve years earlier, in his first inaugural address: "The only thing we have to fear is fear itself." In his final words, FDR recaptures the spirit of optimism and self-confidence that brought the country through the Great Depression and the war. Now, finally, the future of the country seemed positive; peace and prosperity seemed eminently achievable.

The massive stones in this final room are primeval in character and speak to universal human experiences. Their quality is archetypal: they strive to evoke through their shapes and forms essential and basic feelings of energy and awe. The walls are reminiscent of early human habitations and ancient religious constructions. They surround and enclose the room, their flared corners implying strength, permanence, and, therefore, security. On these great, evocative granite walls, FDR's quotations—which summarize the principles that were so vital to the president's hopes for the future—take on a more powerful and inspiring voice.

In the final fountain, huge stones are stacked on each other as if deposited by natural force. The largest of these stones weighs thirty-five tons. Many of the stones are covered by water.

126

WITH STRONG AND ACTIVE FAITH."

The space that is formed by these massive stone walls evolves into the shape of an amphitheater, bounded on the east by a series of seating steps. The seats face inward and focus on the stagelike fountain. A time line of major events in President Roosevelt's life is carved on the risers of these seats.

January 30, 1882	FRANKLIN DELANO ROOSEVELT BORN AT HYDE PARK, NEW YORK
1905	MARRIES ANNA ELEANOR ROOSEVELT
1921	STRICKEN WITH POLIOMYELITIS, ROOSEVELT NEVER AGAIN WALKED UNAIDED
1928–1932	GOVERNOR OF NEW YORK
1932	PLEDGES A "NEW DEAL" FOR THE AMERICAN PEOPLE
1932	ELECTED THIRTY-SECOND PRESIDENT OF THE UNITED STATES
1933	DELIVERS FIRST "FIRESIDE CHAT"
1936	REELECTED TO SECOND TERM AS PRESIDENT
1940	REELECTED TO THIRD TERM AS PRESIDENT
1941	JAPAN ATTACKS PEARL HARBOR—WAR IS DECLARED
1941	GERMANY AND ITALY DECLARE WAR ON THE UNITED STATES
1944	REELECTED TO FOURTH TERM AS PRESIDENT
April 12, 1945	DIES AT WARM SPRINGS, GEORGIA

The fountain in this room is dramatic, inspiring, and involving.

Beyond, across the Tidal Basin, are anchoring views of the Washington Monument and the dome of the Jefferson Memorial. This space within the amphitheater reflects FDR's commitment to communication and information. The amphitheater creates a sense of community where people can join together for mutual involvement. Seated together in this final room, visitors can review the events of FDR's presidency and relate their personal memories and family stories from those incredible years. There is an atmosphere of celebration in this room as well, and visitors can feel vicariously the creative explosion of energy that invigorated the country after the war.

Enormous stones channel cascades of water that plunge into a large pool where megalithic stepping stones invite visitors to interact with their surroundings. The fountain incites feelings of expansiveness and energy. These responses are reminiscent of those feelings felt throughout the country when, finally, we emerged from the long years of depression and war and felt that endless opportunity lie ahead. The large scale and exuberance of the room and the fountain also reflect FDR's own personality and the grandeur of his accomplishments.

An aerial view of the
FDR study model
shows the careful
attention given to the
water effects.

129

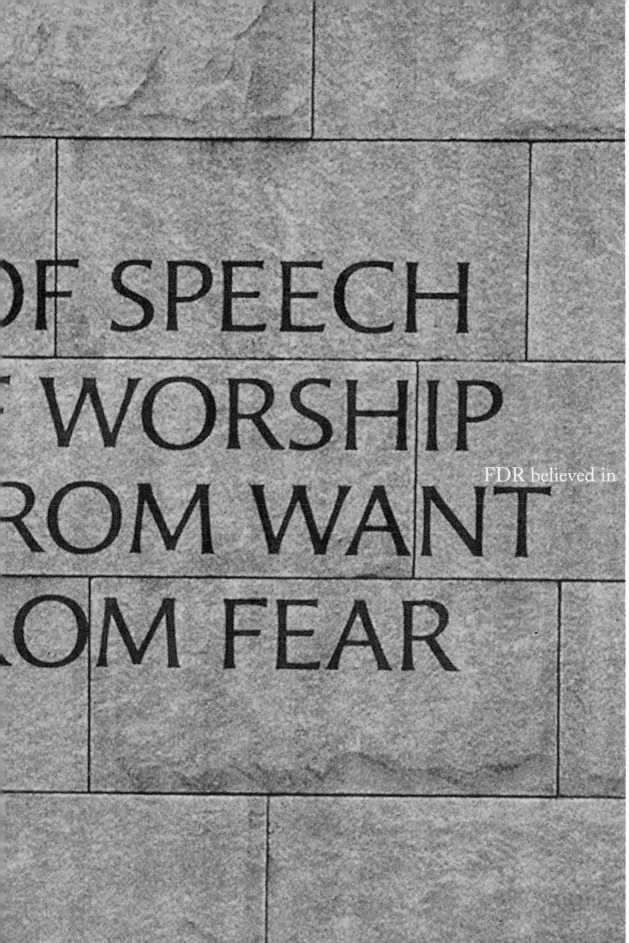

OF SPEECH

WORSHIP

ROM WANT

OM FEAR

As visitors turn away from this final experience, the view explodes outward, toward the whole of Washington and the other memorials that provide a historic context for the FDR presidency. In this vista, there is a tremendous sense of the whole and a realization that each person and event in this nation has contributed to our present experience of the United States.

FDR believed in the American people.

He believed in their capacity to accomplish what needed to be done. He believed that if they were given the right information, they would make the right decisions and the right choices. He believed that the role of a leader was to ensure that people were well and correctly informed. For this to work, people had to be free, and FDR felt that freedom lay at the core of democracy. That was what World War II was all about. That was what we had fought for so long and so hard. FDR defined his hope for the future on January 6, 1941, during his annual message to the Congress. The Memorial ends with that goal, perhaps the most important and enduring of the FDR presidency, the four freedoms: "Freedom of speech, freedom of worship, freedom from want, freedom from fear."

American troops celebrate the peace! May 1945.

The FDR Memorial Teams

Design Team

OFFICE OF LAWRENCE HALPRIN, INC. Lawrence Halprin, Paul Scardina, Susan Aitken, Brian Laczko, Larry Schadt, Dan Morris, Steve Koch, Lisa Kramer, Mike Zisk, Dai Williams, Sue Yung Li Ikeda, Don Carter, and many others who have contributed over a twenty-five-year period.

Design Team Consultants

Adamson Associates, Cost Estimators
Befu Morris Scardina, Consulting Landscape Architects
CMS Collaborative, Fountain Electrical & Mechanical
Flack and Kurtz Engineers, Mechanical Engineering
GFDS Engineering, Structural Engineering
GL and A Civil Engineers, Civil Engineering
Heller and Metzger, Specifications
Marquis Associates, Architectural Consultant for Entry Building
Patrick Quigley and Associates, Lighting
Paul Meyer, Plant Consultant
Schnabel Engineering Associates, Geotechnical Engineers
Smith and Faass Consulting, Electrical Engineering
The Engineering Enterprise, Electrical Engineering
Wiss Janney Elstner, Granite and Waterproofing Specialists

Sculpture Team

Leonard Baskin
John Benson, Stone Carver
Neil Estern
Robert Graham
Tom Hardy
George Segal

National Park Service Teams

National Capital Region: John Parsons, Glenn DeMarr
National Park Service Central: Arnie Goldstein
National Park Service Construction Team: Thomas FitzPatrick
National Park Service Denver Service Center Team:
    Mike Donnelly, Glenn Lamoree, Ed Tafoya

Granite and Construction Teams

Cold Spring Granite, Granite Supplier
Halka Nursery
Independent Construction, Inc., Stone Contractor
Walsh Construction Company, Inc., General Contractor

THEY (WHO) SEEK TO ESTABLISH
SYSTEMS OF GOVERNMENT BASED ON
THE REGIMENTATION OF ALL HUMAN
BEINGS BY A HANDFUL OF INDIVIDUAL
RULERS... CALL THIS A NEW ORDER.
IT IS NOT NEW AND IT IS NOT ORDER.

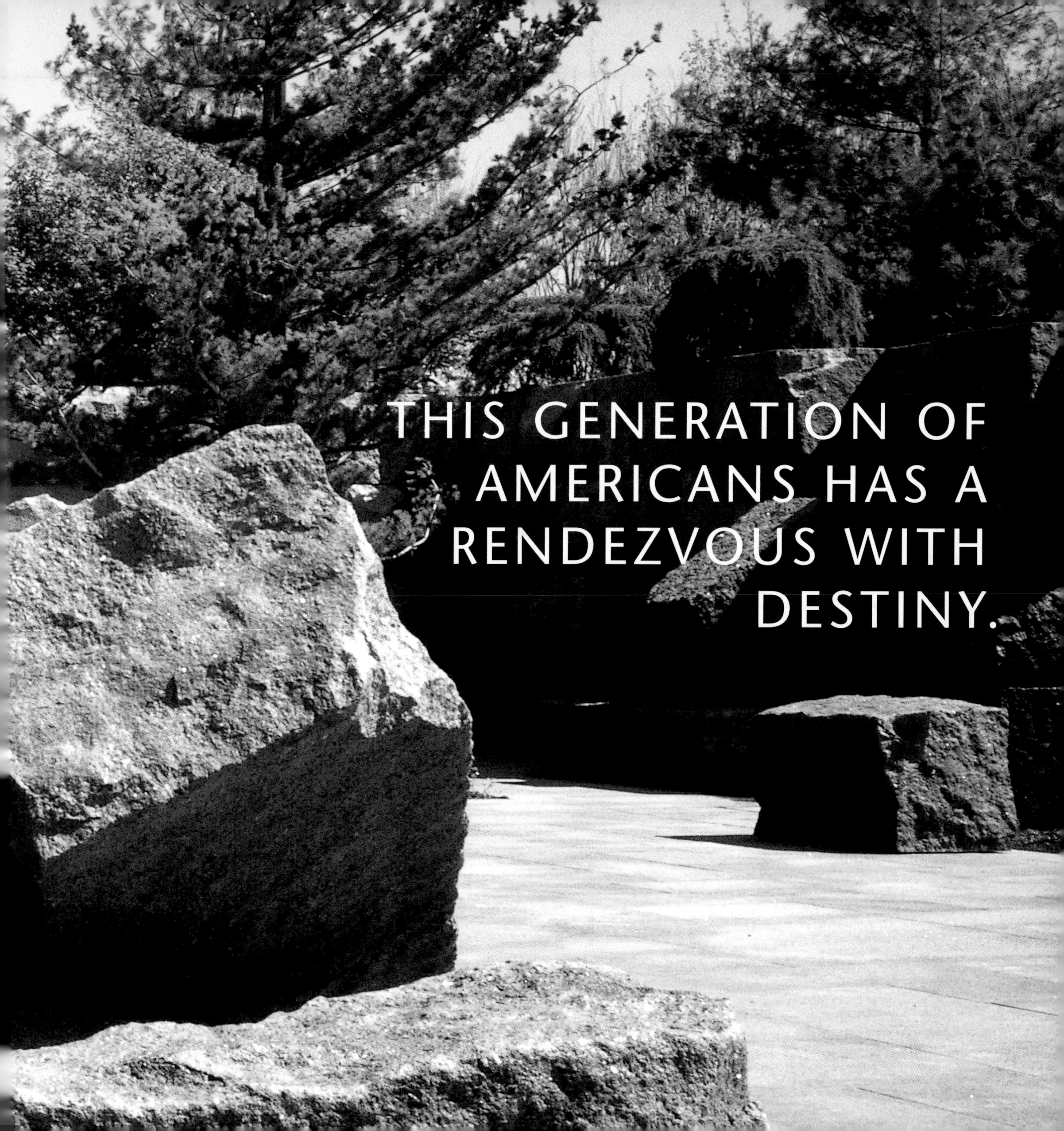

THIS GENERATION OF
AMERICANS HAS A
RENDEZVOUS WITH
DESTINY.